Math Grade 5

Table of Contents

How to Use This Book

1. This book can be used in a home or classroom setting. Read through each unit before working with the student(s). Familiarize yourself with the vocabulary and the skills that are introduced at the top of each unit activity page. Use this information as a guide to help instruct the student(s).

2. Choose a quiet place with little or no interruptions (including the telephone). Talk with the student(s) about the purpose of this book and how you will be working as a team to prepare for standardized tests.

3. As an option, copy the unit test and give it as a pretest to identify weak areas.

4. Upon the completion of each unit, you will find a unit test. Discuss the Helping Hand strategy for test taking featured on the test. Use the example on each test as a chance to show the student(s) how to work through a problem and completely fill in the answer circle. Encourage the student(s) to work independently when possible, but this is a learning time and questions should be welcomed. A time limit is given for each test. Instruct the student(s) to use the time allowed efficiently, looking back over the answers if possible. Tell him to continue until he sees the stop sign.

5. Record the score on the record sheet on page 4. If a student has difficulty with any questions, use the cross-reference guide on the inside back cover to identify the skills that need to be reviewed.

Teach & Test

Introduction

Now this makes sense—teaching our students the skills and strategies that are expected of them before they are tested!

Many students, parents, and teachers are concerned that standardized test scores do not adequately reflect a child's capabilities. This may be due to one or more of the factors italicized below. The purpose of this book is to reduce the negative impact of these, or similar factors, on a student's standardized test scores. The goal is to target those factors and alter their effects as described.

1. *The student has been taught the tested skills but has forgotten them.* This book is divided into units that are organized similarly to fifth grade textbooks. Instructions for the skill itself are found at the top of each unit activity page, ensuring that the student has been exposed to each key component. The exercises include drill/practice and creative learning activities. Additional activity suggestions can be found in a star burst within the units. These activities require the students to apply the skills that they are practicing.

2. *The student has mastered the skills but has never seen them presented in a test-type format.* Ideally, the skills a student learns at school will be used as part of problem solving in the outside world. For this reason, the skills in this book, and in most classrooms, are not practiced in a test-type format. At the end of each unit in this book, the skills are specifically matched with test questions. In this way, the book serves as a type of "bridge" between the skills that the student(s) has mastered and the standardized test format.

3. *The student is inexperienced with the answer sheet format.* Depending on the standardized test that your school district uses, students are expected to use a fill-in-the-bubble name grid and score sheet. To familiarize students with this process, a name grid and score sheet are included for the review tests found at the midway point and again at the end of the book.

4. *The student may feel the anxiety of a new and unfamiliar situation.* While testing, students will notice changes in their daily routine: their classroom door will be closed with a "Testing" sign on it, children will be asked not to use the restroom, their desks may be separated, their teacher may read from a script and refuse to repeat herself, etc. To help relieve the stress caused by these changes, treat each unit test in this book as it would be treated at school by following the procedures listed below.

Stage a Test

You will find review tests midway through the book and again at the end of the book. When you reach these points, "stage a test" by creating a real test-taking environment. The procedures listed below coincide with many standardized test directions. The purpose is to alleviate stress, rather than contribute to it, so make this a serious, but calm, event and the student(s) will benefit.

1. Prepare! Have the student(s) sharpen two pencils, lay out scratch paper, and use the restroom.

2. Choose a room with a door that can be closed. Ask a student to put a sign on the door that reads "Testing" and explain that no talking will be permitted after the sign is hung.

3. Direct the student(s) to turn to a specific page but not to begin until the instructions are completely given.

4. Read the instructions at the top of the page and work through the example together. Discuss the Helping Hand strategy that is featured at the top of the page. Have the student(s) neatly and completely fill in the bubble for the example. This is the child's last chance to ask for help!

5. Instruct the student(s) to continue working until the stop sign is reached. If a student needs help reading, you may read each question only once.

Helping Hand Test Strategies

The first page of each test features a specific test-taking strategy that will be helpful in working through most standardized tests. These strategies are introduced and spotlighted one at a time so that they will be learned and remembered internally. Each will serve as a valuable test-taking tool, so discuss them thoroughly.

The strategies include:

- Sometimes the correct answer is not given. Fill in the circle beside NG if no answer is correct.
- Always read each question carefully.
- Read all the answer choices before you decide.
- If you are not sure what the answer is, skip it and come back to it later.
- Cross out answers you know are wrong.
- Always read the question twice. Does your answer make sense?
- Take time to review your answers.
- Note the time allotment. Pace yourself.

Constructed-Response Questions

You will find the final question of each test is written in a different format called constructed response. This means that students are not provided with answer choices, but are instead asked to construct their own answers. The objective of such an "open-ended" type of question is to provide students with a chance to creatively develop reasonable answers. It also provides an insight to a student's reasoning and thinking skills. As this format is becoming more accepted and encouraged by standardized test developers, students will be "ahead of the game" by practicing such responses now.

Evaluating the Tests

Two types of questions are included in each test. The unit tests consist of 20 multiple-choice questions, the midway review test consists of 25 multiple-choice questions, and the final review test consists of 30 multiple-choice questions. All tests include a "constructed-response" question which requires the student(s) to construct and sometimes support an answer. Use the following procedures to evaluate a student's performance on each test.

1. Use the answer key found on pages 125–128 to correct the tests. Be sure the student(s) neatly and completely filled in the answer circles.

2. Record the scores on the record sheet found on page 4. If the student(s) incorrectly answered any questions, use the cross-reference guide found on the inside back cover to help identify the skills the student(s) needs to review. Each test question references the corresponding activity page.

3. Scoring the "constructed response" questions is somewhat subjective. Discuss these questions with the student(s). Sometimes it is easier for the student(s) to explain the answer verbally. Help the student to record her thoughts as a written answer. If the student(s) has difficulty formulating a response, refer back to the activity pages using the cross-reference guide. Also review the star burst activity found in the unit which also requires the student(s) to formulate an answer.

4. Discuss the test with the student(s). What strategies were used to answer the questions? Were some questions more difficult than others? Was there enough time? What strategies did the student(s) use while taking the test?

Record Sheet

Record a student's score for each test by drawing a star or placing a sticker below each item number that was correct. Leave the incorrect boxes empty as this will allow you to visually see any weak spots. Review and practice those missed skills, then retest only the necessary items.

Unit 1

1	2	3	4	5	6	7	8	9	10	11	12	13	14	15	16	17	18	19	20

Unit 2

1	2	3	4	5	6	7	8	9	10	11	12	13	14	15	16	17	18	19	20

Unit 3

1	2	3	4	5	6	7	8	9	10	11	12	13	14	15	16	17	18	19	20

Unit 4

1	2	3	4	5	6	7	8	9	10	11	12	13	14	15	16	17	18	19	20

Midway Review Test

1	2	3	4	5	6	7	8	9	10	11	12	13	14	15	16	17	18	19	20

21	22	23	24	25

Unit 5

1	2	3	4	5	6	7	8	9	10	11	12	13	14	15	16	17	18	19	20

Unit 6

1	2	3	4	5	6	7	8	9	10	11	12	13	14	15	16	17	18	19	20

Unit 7

1	2	3	4	5	6	7	8	9	10	11	12	13	14	15	16	17	18	19	20

Unit 8

1	2	3	4	5	6	7	8	9	10	11	12	13	14	15	16	17	18	19	20

Final Review Test

1	2	3	4	5	6	7	8	9	10	11	12	13	14	15	16	17	18	19	20

21	22	23	24	25	26	27	28	29	30

Place value

billions			millions			thousands			ones		
hundreds	tens	ones	hundreds	tens	ones	hundreds	tens	ones	hundreds	tens	ones
8	4	2	1	9	6	3	4	5	2	0	1

842,196,345,201

eight hundred forty-two billion, one hundred ninety-six million, three hundred forty-five thousand, two hundred one

Write the value of the underlined digit in word form.

1. 7<u>4</u>6,196

fourty thousand

2. <u>8</u>,946,243,000

eight billion

3. 8<u>5</u>2,146,306

fifty million

4. 965,<u>4</u>09

five thousand

5. 3,428,99<u>8</u>

eight

6. <u>7</u>8,456

seventy thous...

7. <u>3</u>,543,192

three million

8. <u>4</u>06,294

four hundred thousand

9. <u>7</u>06,421,599

seven hundred million

10. <u>2</u>,416,349,187

two billion

11. 474,891,17<u>6</u>

six

12. 845,317,764,<u>2</u>49

two hundred

Write each number in word form. Example: 341 = three hundred forty-one

13. 3,421,800,000

three billion, four hundred twenty one million, eight hundred thousand

14. 45,982,406,399

fourty five billion, nine hundred eighty two million, four hundred six thousand, three hundred ninety nine.

Write your own 11-digit numeral. Then write it in word form.

Name

Rounding numbers

Rounding helps estimate, and makes numbers easier to work with when exact answers are not necessary!

Round 8,492,256 to the nearest million.

If the digit after the 8 million is:
    5 or more, round up
    4 or less, round down

Since it is 4 or less, round down.

8,492,256 rounds to 8,000,000

More examples:

Rounding to the nearest thousand:
34,879 rounds to 35,000

Rounding to the nearest ten:
435,182 rounds to 435,180

Rounding to the nearest hundred thousand:
567,234 rounds to 600,000

Round to the nearest hundred dollars.

1. $437.82	2. $589.01	3. $634.08	4. $982.98	5. $648.92
$400	$600	$600	$1,000	$600

Round to the nearest thousand.

6. 8,433	7. 5,421	8. 9,741	9. 5,921	10. 7,438
8,000	5,000	10,000	6,000	7,000

Round to the nearest ten thousand.

11. 64,296	12. 54,989	13. 76,489	14. 38,496	15. 25,492
60,000	50,000	80,000	40,000	30,000

Round to the place of the underlined digit.

16. 1<u>9</u>	17. 3<u>4</u>8	18. <u>6</u>91
20	350	700

19. <u>5</u>47	20. 6,4<u>8</u>2	21. 7<u>4</u>9
500	6,480	750

22. <u>6</u>92	23. 3,<u>4</u>21	24. 6<u>9</u>8,412
700	3,400	700,000

25. 3<u>6</u>4,412	26. <u>7</u>2,496	27. <u>3</u>49,064
360,000	70,000	300,000

Comparing and ordering numbers

Unit 1

When comparing two numbers, examine their place values:

45,231

45,729

Where do the two numbers begin to differ in value?

Examine each digit: 200 < 700

So: 45,231 < 45,729

45,231 is less than 45,729.

Another example:

862,241

857,372

The ten thousands are the first digits to differ in value.

60,000 > 50,000

So: 86,241 > 857,372

Compare the numbers using > or <.

1. 64 ⟨>⟩ 27

2. 506 ⟨>⟩ 56

3. 641 ⟨>⟩ 461

4. 48 ⟨<⟩ 84

5. 728 ⟨<⟩ 782

6. 5,491 ⟨<⟩ 5,941

7. 8,463 ⟨>⟩ 6,891

8. 9,485 ⟨>⟩ 5,849

9. 74,912 ⟨>⟩ 43,819

10. 83,214 ⟨>⟩ 83,211

11. 54,295 ⟨<⟩ 82,918

12. 924,146 ⟨<⟩ 948,862

Order each set of numbers from least to greatest.

13. 8,241; 942; 6,597; 192

192, 942, 6597, 8241

14. 8,297; 5,495; 929; 1,382

929, 1382, 5495, 8297

15. 92,149; 42,394; 92,140

42394, 92140, 92149

16. 342,192; 928,191; 340,384

340384, 342192, 928191

17. 80,492; 849,142; 8,298

8298, 80492, 849142

7

Addition of greater numbers
Unit 1

Add the ones. Regroup.	Add the tens. Regroup.	Add the hundreds. Regroup.	Add the thousands.
1 4,836 + 1,987 3	1 1 4,836 + 1,987 23	1 1 1 4,836 + 1,987 823	1 1 1 4,836 + 1,987 6,823

Solve the problems.

REGROUP

1. 3,421
   + 9,947
     13,368

2. 6,429
   + 1,843
     8,272

3. 9,249
   + 2,137
     +0386
     16,386

4. 5,429
   + 3,870
     9,299

5. 6,484
   + 2,929
     9,413

6. 7,642
   + 1,859
     9,501

7. 7,298
   + 2,846
     10,144

8. 5,421
   + 8,298
     13,719

9. 6,489
   + 2,576
     9,065

10. 3,465
   + 2,987
     6,452

11. 5,642
   + 2,987
     8,629

12. 3,841
   + 2,839
     6,680

13. 34,215
   + 25,398
     59,613

14. 319,648
   + 81,349
     400,997

15. 72,817
   + 139,798
     212,615

16. 67,918
   + 38,217
     106,135

Subtraction of greater numbers

Borrow and regroup. Subtract the ones.	Borrow and regroup. Subtract the tens.	Borrow and regroup. Subtract the hundreds.	Borrow and regroup. Subtract the thousands.	Subtract the ten thousands. Add the comma.
3 15 62,1̶4̶8̶ − 28,356 9	0 13 15 62,1̶4̶5̶ − 28,356 89	1 10 13 15 6̶2̶,1̶4̶8̶ − 28,356 789	5 11 10 13 15 6̶2̶,1̶4̶8̶ − 28,356 3789	5 11 10 13 15 6̶2̶,1̶4̶8̶ − 28,356 33,789

Subtract. If the difference is even, give it an X. If the difference is odd, give it an O. Play tic-tac-toe.

3,153 − 1,245 4,398	4,528 − 1,392 3,136	7,643 − 2,818 4,825
5,420 − 1,287 4,133	7,645 − 1,829 5,816	3,843 − 1,927 1,916
76,412 − 34,829 41,583	56,218 − 28,303 27,915	89,516 − 28,138 61,378

36,142 − 8,195 27,947	4,219 − 382 3,837	58,418 − 9,312 49,106
3,849 − 1,893 1,956	76,413 − 8,321 68,042	49,218 − 18,309 30,909
92,142 − 8,037 84,105	7,642 − 855 6,787	9,280 − 3,417 5,863

Subtracting with zeroes

When borrowing, you must find a digit with a greater value than zero. Regroup.	Borrow and regroup.	Borrow and regroup.	Subtract.
6 10 7 0̸ 0 2 − 1 8 7 9	9 6 1̸0̸ 10 7 0̸ 0̸ 2 − 1 8 7 9	9 9 6 1̸0̸ 1̸0̸ 12 7 0̸ 0̸ 2̸ − 1 8 7 9	9 9 6 1̸0̸ 1̸0̸ 12 7 0̸ 0̸ 2̸ − 1 8 7 9 ――――― 5,123

Solve the problems.

1.
```
   60
-  28
-----
   32
```

2.
```
   90
-  27
-----
   63
```

3.
```
  400
- 128
-----
  272
```

4.
```
  600
- 248
-----
  352
```

5.
```
  800
- 547
-----
  253
```

6.
```
  200
- 146
-----
   54
```

7.
```
  801
- 342
-----
  459
```

8.
```
  720
- 545
-----
  175
```

9.
```
   50
-  25
-----
   25
```

10.
```
  700
- 568
-----
  132
```

11. ✓
```
  2,040
- 1,829
-------
    211
```

12.
```
  6,090
- 3,867
-------
   2223
```

13.
```
  9,002
- 3,846
-------
   5156
```

14.
```
  300
- 208
-----
   92
```

15.
```
  6,000
- 4,235
-------
   1765
```

16.
```
  605,008
- 123,124
---------
   481884
```

Addition and subtraction of money   Unit 1

Begin by lining up the decimal points. Then add a decimal point into the answer.	Borrow, regroup, and subtract.	Place a dollar sign at the front of your answer.
$600.00 − 264.82 .	9 9 9 5 10 10 10 10 $6̸0̸0̸.0̸0̸ − 264.82 335.18	9 9 9 5 10 10 10 10 $6̸0̸0̸.0̸0̸ − 264.82 $335.18

Add. Don't forget your decimal point and dollar sign in the sum.

1. $ 50.32
   + 24.89
   $75.21

2. $64.21
   + 23.49
   $87.70

3. $200.00
   + 182.48
   $352.48

4. $64.98
   + 28.23
   $93.21

5. $ 7.42
   + 2.89
   $10.31

6. $80.42
   + 24.58
   $105.00

7. + ✓ $ 6.21
   + 3.48
   $9.69

8. $24.81
   + 25.23
   $50.04

9. $60.40
   + 25.38
   $85.78

10. $724.41
   + 82.53
   $806.94

11. $92.45
   + 8.35
   $100.80

12. $925.33
   + 8.98
   $934.31

Subtract. Don't forget your decimal point and dollar sign in the difference.

13. $ 60.00
   − 3.82
   $56.18

14. $7.08
   − 3.52
   $3.56

15. $500.24
   − 8.13
   $492.11

16. $.89
   − .24
   65¢

17. $ 76.04
   − 9.42
   $66.62

18. $7.00
   − 2.46
   $4.54

19. ✓ $500.00
   − 8.13
   $491.87

20. ✓ $78.42
   − 9.57
   $68.85

21. $84.56
   − 29.87
   54.69

22. $5.00
   + 2.36
   $2.64

23. $17.24
   + 8.13
   $9.11

24. $30.89
   − 9.24
   $21.65

8:30 to

Unit 1 Test

numeration

Read the question. Use an extra piece of paper to write problems down and solve them. Fill in the circle beside the best answer.

☐ Example:

Which set of numbers are ordered correctly from least to greatest?

(A) 3; 214; 86; 456; 21

(B) 81; 801; 8,021; 8

(C) 24; 56; 324; 2,354

(D) NG

Sometimes the correct answer is not given. Fill in the circle beside NG if no answer is correct.

Answer: C because all of the numbers are ordered from least to greatest.

Now try these. You have 20 minutes. Continue until you see ⬡STOP .

---

1. Match the number 3,789,123 with the correct word form.

(A) three thousand, seven hundred eighty-nine

(B) three million, seven hundred eighty-nine thousand, one hundred twenty-three

(C) thirty-seven million, eighty-nine thousand, one hundred twenty-three

(D) NG

---

2. Identify the value of the underlined digit. 56,423

six thousand	six hundred	sixty thousand	six ten thousand
(A)	(B)	(C)	(D)

---

3. Round 345 to its greatest place value.

340	400	300	440
(A)	(B)	(C)	(D)

GO ON ➡

Unit 1 Test

4. Round $456.78 to the nearest hundred dollars.

$500.00	$450.00	$400.00	$550.00
(A)	(B)	(C)	(D)

5. Round 679,234 to the nearest ten thousand.

700,000	670,000	600,000	680,000
(A)	(B)	(C)	(D)

6. Order the following numbers correctly from least to greatest: 576; 34; 3,124; 5

(A) 576; 34; 3,124; 5   (B) 5; 34; 576; 3,124

(C) 34; 576; 5; 3,124   (D) 5; 34; 3,124; 576

7. Compare the numbers using >, <, or =.

7,869 ◯ 789

(A) >   (B) <
(C) =   (D) NG

8.
$625.52
+ 706.93
1,332.65

$1,432.47	$1,912.45	$1,332.45	$1,532.54
(A)	(B)	(C)	(D)

9. Which problem is regrouped correctly after adding the ones column?

3 395 + 238 1	0 6,421 + 2,849 1	5 37 + 28 1	NG
(A)	(B)	(C)	(D)

10.
24,652
+ 13,896
38,548

36,499	38,548	37,498	10,756
(A)	(B)	(C)	(D)

GO ON

Name

11. What is the missing digit?

3,426
+ 1,8☐3
5,279

8 (A)   3 (B)   6 (C)   NG (D)

12. Which digit should be used to make this problem correct?

1 1
6,481
3,824
+ 2,3☐3
12,638

4 (A)   6 (B)   3 (C)   5 (D)

13.

⁸¹⁶
396
– 278
118

120 (A)   118 (B)   119 (C)   674 (D)

14. Which number will make this problem correct?

689
– ☐
223

466 (A)   367 (B)   525 (C)   912 (D)

15.

⁶ ¹⁰ ¹ ¹⁴
7,024
– 3,819
3,205

4,824 (A)   3,205 (B)   4,819 (C)   10,843 (D)

16. Which column is subtracted incorrectly?

8 12 3 16
39,246
– 18,938
20,408

(A) ones column   (B) hundreds column
(C) thousands column   (D) ten thousands column

GO ON

17.
5 9 10
6,000
− 2,147
4853

3,859 Ⓐ 4,857 Ⓑ 4,147 Ⓒ 3,853 Ⓓ

18.
300
− 196

296 Ⓐ 157 Ⓑ 104 Ⓒ 496 Ⓓ

19.
$50.25
−   8.19

$42.06 Ⓐ $52.19 Ⓑ $8.19 Ⓒ $58.44 Ⓓ

20. Which problem is correct?

| $18.97 + 7.23 = $26.20 Ⓐ | $189.7 + 7.23 = $26.20 Ⓑ | $1.897 + 7.23 = $26.20 Ⓒ | NG Ⓓ |

Where is a common place that you hear "rounded numbers" being used all the time?

The place I hear rounded number a lot is time

The properties of multiplication

$3 \times 9 = 9 \times 3$
Commutative Property (Changing the order of the factors does not change the product.)

$6 \times (3 \times 9) = (6 \times 3) \times 9$
Associative Property (Changing how you group the factors does not change the product.)

$(3 \times 2) + (3 \times 6) = 3 \times (2 + 6)$
Distributive Property (When the sum equals two products being multiplied by the same factor, simply find the sum of the other two factors and multiply by the common factor.)

$0 \times 7 = 0$
Zero Property (When you multiply any factor by zero, the product is always equal to zero.)

$1 \times 9 = 9$
Property of One (When you multiply a factor by one, the product is always equal to the amount of the other factor.)

Identify each property.

1. $3 \times 0 = 0$
   zero property

2. $(3 \times 6) \times 1 = 3 \times (6 \times 1)$
   associative property

3. $9 \times 2 = 2 \times 9$
   commutative Property

4. $6 \times 1 = 6$
   property of one

5. $(7 \times 3) + (7 \times 5) = 7 \times (3 + 5)$
   distributive property

6. $(7 \times 5) \times 6 = 7 \times (5 \times 6)$
   associative

7. $3 \times 7 = 7 \times 3$
   commutative Property

8. $(3 \times 6) \times 1 = 3 \times (6 \times 1)$
   associative Property

9. $(8 \times 4) + (8 \times 9) = 8 \times (4 + 9)$
   distributive Property

Find the value of n.

10. $(n \times 3) + (7 \times 4) = n \times (3 + 4)$ n = ___7___

11. $3 \times n = 8 \times 3$ n = ___8___

12. $9 \times n = 0$ n = ___0___

13. $(n \times 4) \times 3 = 7 \times (4 \times 3)$ n = ___7___

14. $n \times 4 = 4$ n = ___1___

15. $(5 \times 3) + (n \times 7) = 5 \times (3 + 7)$ n = ___5___

16. $(n \times 2) + (n \times 8) = 7 \times (2 + 8)$ n = ___7___

COMMUTATIVE PROPERTY

Multiplying by 1-digit numbers

Unit 2

Multiply the ones column. Regroup.

```
        1
     4,232
  x      6
         2
```

Multiply the remaining columns. Regroup as necessary.

```
    1 1 1
     4,232
  x      6
    25,392
```

Multiply.

1.
```
     94
  x   3
    282
```

2.
```
     24
  x   7
    168
```

3.
```
     36
  x   9
    324
```

4.
```
     37
  x   5
    185
```

5.
```
     59
  x   8
    427
```

6.
```
    316
  x   2
    632
```

7.
```
    428
  x   3
   1284
```

8.
```
    712
  x   7
   4984
```

9.
```
    413
  x   5
   2065
```

10.
```
    324
  x   6
   1944
```

11.
```
    434
  x   6
   2604
```

12.
```
    894
  x   3
   2682
```

13.
```
    486
  x   7
   3402
```

14.
```
    658
  x   5
   3290
```

15.
```
    647
  x   8
   5176
```

16.
```
   3,143
  x    2
   6286
```

17.
```
   1,231
  x    6
   7386
```

18.
```
   4,824
  x    8
  38592
```

19.
```
   8,132
  x    4
  32528
```

20.
```
   2,108
  x    7
  14756
```

Name

When multiplying by these numbers, begin by multiplying the factors other than zero.
Next, simply add the number of zeroes in the problem to the product.

| Multiply the factors other than zero. | $\begin{array}{r} 3 \\ \times\ 3 \\ \hline 9 \end{array}$ | $\begin{array}{r} 3,000 \\ \times\ \ \ \ 3 \\ \hline \end{array}$ | Add the zeroes in the problem to the product. | $\begin{array}{r} 3,000 \\ \times\ \ \ \ 3 \\ \hline 9 \end{array}$ | $\begin{array}{r} 3,000 \\ \times\ \ \ \ 3 \\ \hline 9,000 \end{array}$ |

Multiply.

1. $\begin{array}{r} 200 \\ \times\ \ \ 30 \\ \hline 6000 \end{array}$

2. $\begin{array}{r} 400 \\ \times\ \ \ 9 \\ \hline 3600 \end{array}$

3. $\begin{array}{r} 50 \\ \times\ \ 8 \\ \hline 400 \end{array}$

4. $\begin{array}{r} 6 \\ \times\ \ 500 \\ \hline 3000 \end{array}$

5. $\begin{array}{r} 200 \\ \times\ \ \ 22 \\ \hline 4400 \end{array}$

6. $\begin{array}{r} 500 \\ \times\ \ \ 8 \\ \hline 4000 \end{array}$

7. $\begin{array}{r} 2,000 \\ \times\ \ \ \ 9 \\ \hline 18,000 \end{array}$

8. $\begin{array}{r} 400 \\ \times\ \ \ 30 \\ \hline 12000 \end{array}$

9. $\begin{array}{r} 300 \\ \times\ \ 200 \\ \hline 60,000 \end{array}$

10. $\begin{array}{r} 500 \\ \times\ \ \ 40 \\ \hline 5000 \end{array}$

11. $\begin{array}{r} 600 \\ \times\ \ \ 3 \\ \hline 18000 \end{array}$

12. $\begin{array}{r} 400 \\ \times\ \ \ 20 \\ \hline 8,000 \end{array}$

13. $\begin{array}{r} 600 \\ \times\ \ \ 60 \\ \hline 36,000 \end{array}$

14. $\begin{array}{r} 8,000 \\ \times\ \ \ \ 20 \\ \hline 160,000 \end{array}$

15. $\begin{array}{r} 2,000 \\ \times\ \ \ \ 22 \\ \hline 44,000 \end{array}$

16. $\begin{array}{r} 50 \\ \times\ \ 50 \\ \hline 2,500 \end{array}$

17. $\begin{array}{r} 20 \\ \times\ \ 700 \\ \hline 14,000 \end{array}$

18. $\begin{array}{r} 1,000 \\ \times\ \ \ \ 45 \\ \hline 45,000 \end{array}$

19. $\begin{array}{r} 200 \\ \times\ \ \ 80 \\ \hline 16,000 \end{array}$

20. $\begin{array}{r} 400 \\ \times\ 2,000 \\ \hline 800,000 \end{array}$

Name _____

Multiplying 2-digit numbers   Unit 2

Multiply by the ones digit. Place a zero in the ones column.	Multiply by the tens digit.	Add.

```
      3
     29
  x  34
  ─────
    116
      0
```

```
     ̷32
     29
  x  34
  ─────
    116
    870
```

```
     ̷32
     29
  x  34
  ─────
    116
  + 870
  ─────
    986
```

Multiply.

1.
```
    41
  x 32
  ────
  1312
```

2.
```
    35
  x 24
  ────
   840
```

3.
```
    21
  x 34
  ────
   714
```

4.
```
    42
  x 16
  ────
   672
```

5.
```
    21
  x 52
  ────
  1,092
```

6.
```
    23
  x 31
  ────
   713
```

7.
```
    21
  x 25
  ────
   525
```

8.
```
    48
  x 12
  ────
   576
```

9.
```
    23
  x 44
  ────
  1012
```

10.
```
    27
  x 18
  ────
   486
```

11.
```
    49
  x 35
  ────
  1,715
```

12.
```
    35
  x 29
  ────
  1,015
```

13.
```
    25
  x 72
  ────
  1,800
```

14.
```
    28
  x 13
  ────
   364
```

15.
```
    98
  x 20
  ────
  1960
```

16.
```
    36
  x 54
  ────
  1944
```

17.
```
    48
  x 62
  ────
  2976
```

18.
```
    28
  x 91
  ────
  2548
```

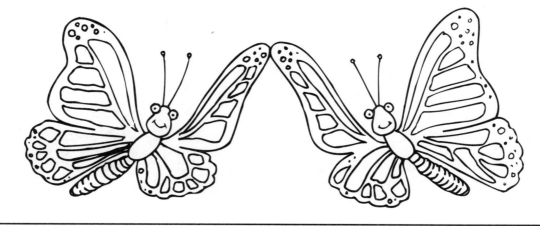

Multiplying 3- and 4-digit numbers

Unit 2

Multiply by the ones digit. Regroup as needed. Place a zero in the ones column.

```
      21
   2,153
 x    54
   8612
      0
```

Multiply by the tens digit. Regroup as needed.

```
      21
      21
   2,153
 x    54
    8612
  107650
```

Add.

```
      21
      21
   2,153
 x    54
    8612
+ 107650
  116,262
```

Solve the problems.

Across:

1.
```
   1,289
 x    30
  38670
```

3.
```
     648
 x    42
   27216
```

6.
```
   6,135
 x    42
  257670
```

8.
```
   1,825
 x    23
  41975
```

10.
```
     698
 x    18
  12564
```

13.
```
     147
 x    27
   3969
```

14.
```
     316
 x    27
   8532
```

15.
```
   1,245
 x    63
  78435
```

Down:

2.
```
     358
 x    24
   8592
```

4.
```
   1,718
 x    46
  79028
```

5.
```
   3,214
 x    21
  67494
```

7.
```
   2,314
 x    31
  71734
```

9.
```
     982
 x    60
  58920
```

10.
```
     217
 x    63
  13671
```

11.
```
   3,245
 x    20
  44900
```

12.
```
     256
 x    19
   4864
```

20

Name _____

Multiplying by 3-digit numbers   Unit 2

Multiply by the ones digit. Regroup as needed. Place a zero in the ones column.

Multiply by the tens digit. Regroup as needed. Place a zero in the tens column and ones column.

Multiply by the hundreds digit. Regroup as needed. Add.

```
    3                  2                 1                 1                 1
   318              318               318               318               318
x  234           x  234            x  234            x  234            x  234
  1272             1272              1272              1272              1272
     0             9540              9540              9540              9540
                     00             63600            +63600            +63600
                                                     74,412            74,412
```

Multiply.

1.
```
   123
x  315
 38,745
```

2.
```
   209
x  354
 73,986
```

3.
```
   352
x  418
147,136
```

4.
```
   295
x  342
100,890
```

5.
```
   302
x  418
126,236
```

6.
```
   204
x  389
 79,356
```

7.
```
   285
x  721
205,485
```

8.
```
   246
x  319
 78,474
```

9.
```
   843
x  300
252,900
```

10.
```
   749
x  123
 92,127
```

11.
```
   603
x  124
 74,772
```

12.
```
   549
x  256
140,544
```

13.
```
   816
x  249
203,184
```

14.
```
   304
x  203
 61,712
```

15.
```
   200
x  649
129,800
```

Multiplication of money

Multiply and regroup as with a regular multiplication problem.

```
  1 3 1
  ⅩⅩⅩ
$31.42
x     89
  28278
+ 251360
 279638
```

Add the dollar ($) sign and decimal point (.) in the product.

```
  1 3 1
  ⅩⅩⅩ
$31.42
x     89
  28278
+ 251360
$2,796.38
```

Unit 2

Multiply. Add the dollar sign and the decimal point.

1.
```
  $4.89
x     6
$29.34
```

2.
```
 $51.06
x     8
$408.48
```

3.
```
 $49.22
x     3
$147.66
```

4.
```
 $82.56
x     7
$577.92
```

5.
```
  $5.89
x     4
$23.56
```

6.
```
  $3.99
x     5
$19.95
```

7.
```
  $8.41
x    32
$269.12
```

8.
```
  $3.53
x    64
$225.92
```

9.
```
 $41.25
x    39
$1608.75
```

10.
```
  $8.86
x    74
$655.64
```

11.
```
  $ .98
x    48
$47.04
```

12.
```
  $ .59
x    76
$44.84
```

13.
```
  $4.86
x    27
$131.22
```

14.
```
 $38.48
x    19
$731.12
```

15.
```
  $8.58
x    23
$197.34
```

16.
```
 $46.92
x    17
$79364
```

17.
```
  $ .42
x    89
$37.38
```

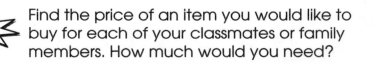

Find the price of an item you would like to buy for each of your classmates or family members. How much would you need?

Name

Estimation
Unit 2

Round each dollar amount to the nearest dollar. Round bottom factors to greatest place value. If single digit, do not round.

	Multiply.	Find the exact answer.	Compare the two.

$$\begin{array}{r} \$38.61 \\ \times \quad 8 \\ \hline \end{array} = \begin{array}{r} \$39 \\ \times \quad 8 \\ \hline \end{array}$$

Multiply.
$$\begin{array}{r} 7 \\ \$39 \\ \times \quad 8 \\ \hline \$312 \end{array}$$ 4 3

Find the exact answer.
$$\begin{array}{r} \$38.61 \\ \times \quad 8 \\ \hline \$308.88 \end{array}$$

Compare the two.
$312 $308.88

Estimate. Find the answer. Compare.

1.
$$\begin{array}{r} \$3.89 \\ \times \quad 24 \\ \hline \$93.36 \end{array} = \begin{array}{r} \$4 \\ \times \quad 20 \\ \hline \$80 \end{array}$$

2.
$$\begin{array}{r} \$8.43 \\ \times \quad 7 \\ \hline \$59.01 \end{array} = \begin{array}{r} \$8.00 \\ \times \quad 7 \\ \hline \$56.00 \end{array}$$

3.
$$\begin{array}{r} \$8.94 \\ \times \quad 62 \\ \hline \$554.28 \end{array} = \begin{array}{r} \$9.00 \\ \times \quad 60 \\ \hline \$5\,0,000 \end{array}$$

4.
$$\begin{array}{r} \$2.79 \\ \times \quad 9 \\ \hline 540 \end{array} = \begin{array}{r} \$3.00 \\ \times \quad 10 \\ \hline \$30.00 \end{array}$$

5.
$$\begin{array}{r} \$16.67 \\ \times \quad 21 \\ \hline \$350.07 \end{array} = \begin{array}{r} \$20 \\ \times \quad 20 \\ \hline 400 \end{array}$$

6.
$$\begin{array}{r} \$48.72 \\ \times \quad 8 \\ \hline \$389.76 \end{array} = \begin{array}{r} \$50 \\ \times \quad 8 \\ \hline \$400 \end{array}$$

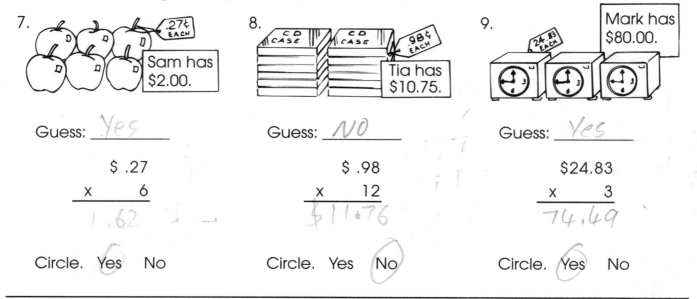

Do they have enough to buy each item? Estimate. Find the actual amount.

7.
.27¢ EACH
Sam has $2.00.

Guess: _Yes_

$$\begin{array}{r} \$ .27 \\ \times \quad 6 \\ \hline 1.62 \end{array}$$

Circle.   Yes   No

8.
CD CASE   CD CASE
.98¢ EACH
Tia has $10.75.

Guess: _NO_

$$\begin{array}{r} \$ .98 \\ \times \quad 12 \\ \hline \$11.76 \end{array}$$

Circle.   Yes   (No)

9.
24.83 EACH
Mark has $80.00.

Guess: _Yes_

$$\begin{array}{r} \$24.83 \\ \times \quad 3 \\ \hline 74.49 \end{array}$$

Circle.   (Yes)   No

Name _____ PY 1-4

Read the question. Use an extra piece of paper
to write problems down and solve them.
Fill in the circle beside the best answer.

☐ Example:

What is the value of n?

(n x 6) + (n x 3) = 7 x (6 + 3)

uz
9   6   7   3
(A)   (B)   (C)   (D)

Answer: C because the Distributive Property multiplies
the common factor by the sum of the other two factors.

Now try these. You have 20 minutes. Continue until you see 〈STOP〉.

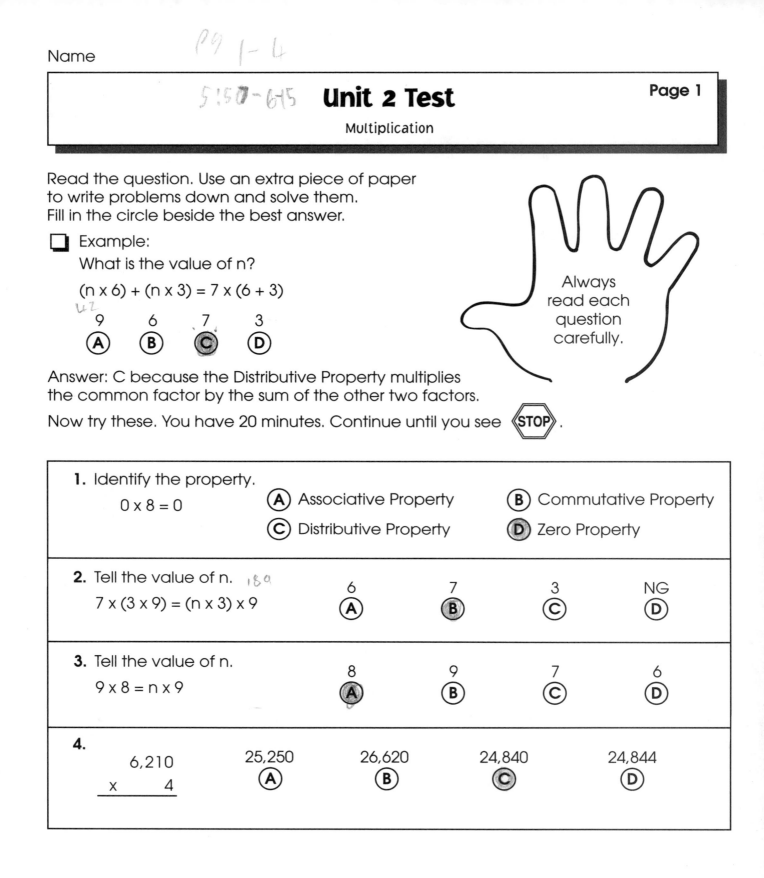

Always
read each
question
carefully.

1. Identify the property. $0 \times 8 = 0$	(A) Associative Property (C) Distributive Property		(B) Commutative Property (D) Zero Property

2. Tell the value of n. 18a
$7 \times (3 \times 9) = (n \times 3) \times 9$

6	7	3	NG
(A)	(B)	(C)	(D)

3. Tell the value of n.
$9 \times 8 = n \times 9$

8	9	7	6
(A)	(B)	(C)	(D)

4.
```
    6,210
x       4
```

25,250	26,620	24,840	24,844
(A)	(B)	(C)	(D)

GO ON

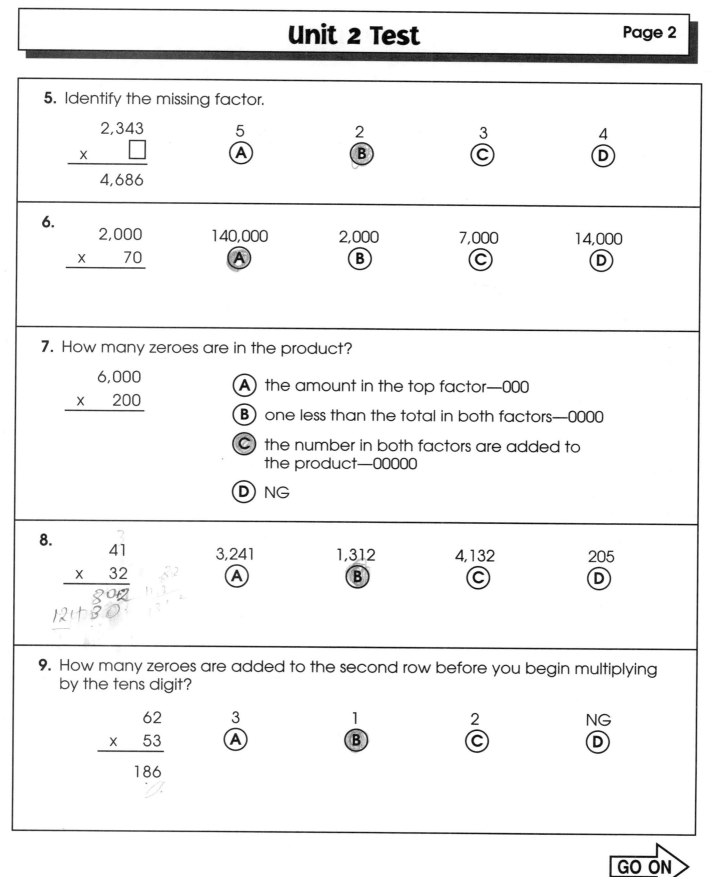

5. Identify the missing factor.

```
  2,343
x     □
-------
  4,686
```

(A) 5   (B) 2   (C) 3   (D) 4

6.

```
  2,000
x    70
```

(A) 140,000   (B) 2,000   (C) 7,000   (D) 14,000

7. How many zeroes are in the product?

```
  6,000
x   200
```

(A) the amount in the top factor—000

(B) one less than the total in both factors—0000

(C) the number in both factors are added to the product—00000

(D) NG

8.

```
    41
x   32
------
```

(A) 3,241   (B) 1,312   (C) 4,132   (D) 205

9. How many zeroes are added to the second row before you begin multiplying by the tens digit?

```
    62
x   53
------
   186
```

(A) 3   (B) 1   (C) 2   (D) NG

GO ON

10.

3,142
x 23

handwritten: 31,420 / x 2 / 62,940
handwritten: 9426 / 6,2840 / 72,868

31,423	70,215	72,266	NG
(A)	(B)	(C)	(D)

11. After multiplying by the ones digit, how many digits will be in the first row?

1,234
x 52

5	4	3	2
(A)	(B)	(C)	(D)

12. Which row has a multiplication error, causing the product to be incorrect?

345
x   121
─────────
445   row A
6900   row B
+ 34500   row C
─────────
41845

(A) row C
(B) row B
(C) There are no errors.
(D) row A

13.

205
x   314

20,531	60,294	64,370	NG
(A)	(B)	(C)	(D)

14.

$82.91
x   7

$580.37	$820.70	$600.42	$508.37
(A)	(B)	(C)	(D)

GO ON

15. If Solomon buys 3 radios at $23.95 each, is his total greater than, less than, or equal to $75.00?

(A) equal to $75.00   (B) less than $75.00

(C) greater than $75.00   (D) NG

16. What is wrong with this problem?

$8.95
x   72
―――――
1790
62650
―――――
$64.440

(A) There is a multiplication error.

(B) The decimal is incorrectly placed.

(C) The columns are not placed correctly.

(D) NG

17. Which estimate is rounded correctly?

$89.40 x 72	$90 x 72	$89 x 70	$90 x 80	$90 x 70
	(A)	(B)	(C)	(D)

18. According to your estimate, will the product be greater than, less than, or equal to $2,000.00?

$49.85
x   32

(A) equal to $2000.00   (B) less than $2,000.00

(C) greater than $2,000.00   (D) NG

19. Tabitha has $12.00. According to your estimate, how much more money will she need to purchase 2 CDs at $6.99?

$3.00	$2.00	$5.00	NG
(A)	(B)	(C)	(D)

20.

703
x   18

12,654
(A)

12,566
(B)

13,654
(C)

6,327
(D)

Rewrite the problem correctly. Then redo the problem to find the product.

848
x   72

1   6 96
593 6 0

604,2 96

Explain why this product is incorrect.

Number are miss placed and some are

missing

How far off was the product? __543,040__

Name

1-digit quotients with remainders

Unit 3

Is the tens digit great enough to divide into? No. We must divide into the 53 ones.

$$6\overline{)53}$$

How many groups of 6 come closest to equaling 53? 8

$$6\overline{)53}^{\,8}$$

Multiply the partial quotient (8) by the divisor (6) and subtract the product (48) from the dividend.

$$\begin{array}{r} 8 \\ 6\overline{)53} \\ -48 \\ \hline 5 \end{array}$$

Is the difference great enough to divide into? No. It becomes the remainder.

$$\begin{array}{r} 8\ R5 \\ 6\overline{)53} \\ -48 \\ \hline 5 \end{array}$$

Divide.

1. $2\overline{)19}$ 9 R1 18 1

2. $4\overline{)27}$ 6 R3 24 3

3. $5\overline{)44}$ 8 R4 -40 4

4. $3\overline{)17}$ 5 R2 -15 2

5. $6\overline{)45}$ 7 R3 -42 3

6. $7\overline{)60}$ 8 R4 -56 4

7. $8\overline{)75}$ 9 R3 72 3

8. $6\overline{)51}$ 8 R3 48 3

9. $7\overline{)68}$ 9 R5 63 5

10. $4\overline{)35}$ 8 R3 32 3

11. $3\overline{)20}$ 6 R2 18 2

12. $9\overline{)80}$ 8 R8 72 8

13. $8\overline{)68}$ 8 R4 64 4

14. $5\overline{)49}$ 9 R4 45 4

15. $7\overline{)52}$ 7 R3 49 3

16. $8\overline{)60}$ 7 56

2-digit quotients—no remainders

Is the hundreds digit great enough to divide into by 6? No. Divide into the 53 tens. Multiply the partial quotient by the divisor and subtract.

```
      8
6 ) 534
  - 48
      5
```

Is the difference of 5 great enough to divide into? No. Bring down the 4 ones. You now have 54 ones.

```
      8
6 ) 534
  - 48
     54
```

Are the 54 ones great enough to be divided into by 6? Yes. Divide. Multiply the partial quotient by the divisor and subtract.

```
     89
6 ) 534
  - 48
     54
   - 54
      0
```

Are there any more digits to bring down in the dividend? No. You are finished.

```
     89
6 ) 534
  - 48
     54
   - 54
      0
```

Divide.

1. $2 \overline{)196}$

2. $5 \overline{)335}$

3. $7 \overline{)476}$

4. $3 \overline{)273}$

5. $6 \overline{)204}$

6. $8 \overline{)624}$

7. $7 \overline{)182}$

8. $4 \overline{)292}$

9. $8 \overline{)464}$

10. $4 \overline{)324}$

11. $6 \overline{)576}$

12. $3 \overline{)141}$

13. $6 \overline{)174}$

14. $5 \overline{)240}$

15. $9 \overline{)243}$

16. $8 \overline{)232}$

17. $5 \overline{)415}$

18. $7 \overline{)532}$

19. $3 \overline{)123}$

20. $6 \overline{)432}$

Name

2-digit quotients with remainders

Unit 3

Is the hundreds digit great enough to divide into by 7? No. Divide into 58 tens. Multiply the partial quotient by the divisor and subtract.

```
    8
7 ) 586
  - 56
    2
```

Is the difference of 2 great enough to divide into? No. Bring down the 6. Now you have 26 ones.

```
    8
7 ) 586
  - 56
     26
```

Are the 26 ones great enough to divide into? Yes. Divide. Multiply the partial quotient by the divisor and subtract.

```
    83
7 ) 586
  - 56
     26
   - 21
      5
```

Is the difference of 5 great enough to divide into? No. Are there any more digits in the dividend to bring down? No. The difference becomes a remainder.

```
    83 R5
7 ) 586
  - 56
     26
   - 21
      5
```

Divide.

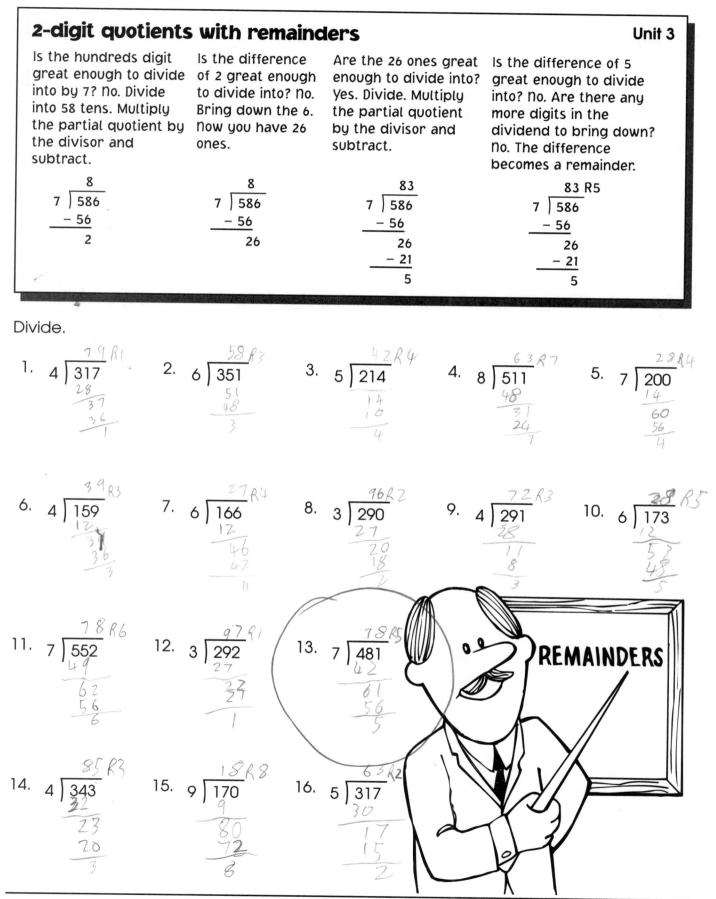

1. 4) 317   79 R1
   28
   37
   36
    1

2. 6) 351   58 R3
   51
   48
    3

3. 5) 214   42 R4
   14
   10
    4

4. 8) 511   63 R7
   48
   31
   24
    7

5. 7) 200   28 R4
   14
   60
   56
    4

6. 4) 159   39 R3
   12
   3
   36
    3

7. 6) 166   27 R4
   12
   46
   42
    4

8. 3) 290   96 R2
   27
   20
   18
    2

9. 4) 291   72 R3
   28
   11
    8
    3

10. 6) 173   28 R5
    12
    53
    48
     5

11. 7) 552   78 R6
    49
    62
    56
     6

12. 3) 292   97 R1
    27
    22
    21
     1

13. 7) 481   78 R5
    42
    61
    56
     5

14. 4) 343   85 R3
    32
    23
    20
     3

15. 9) 170   18 R8
    9
    80
    72
     8

16. 5) 317   63 R2
    30
    17
    15
     2

REMAINDERS

Name

3-digit quotients

Unit 3

Is the hundreds digit great enough to divide into? Yes. Divide. Multiply the partial quotient by the divisor and subtract.

```
      1
  4 ) 543
    - 4
      1
```

Is the difference of 1 great enough to divide into? No. Bring down the 4. Now you have 14. Divide the 14 by the divisor. Multiply and subtract.

```
     13
  4 ) 543
    - 4
     14
   - 12
      2
```

Is the difference of 2 great enough to divide into? No. Bring down the 3. Now you have 23. Divide the 23 by the divisor. Multiply and subtract.

```
    135
  4 ) 543
    - 4
     14
   - 12
     23
   - 20
      3
```

Is the difference of 3 great enough to divide into? No. Are there any more digits to bring down in the dividend? No. The 3 becomes a remainder.

```
   135 R3
  4 ) 543
    - 4
     14
   - 12
     23
   - 20
      3
```

Divide.

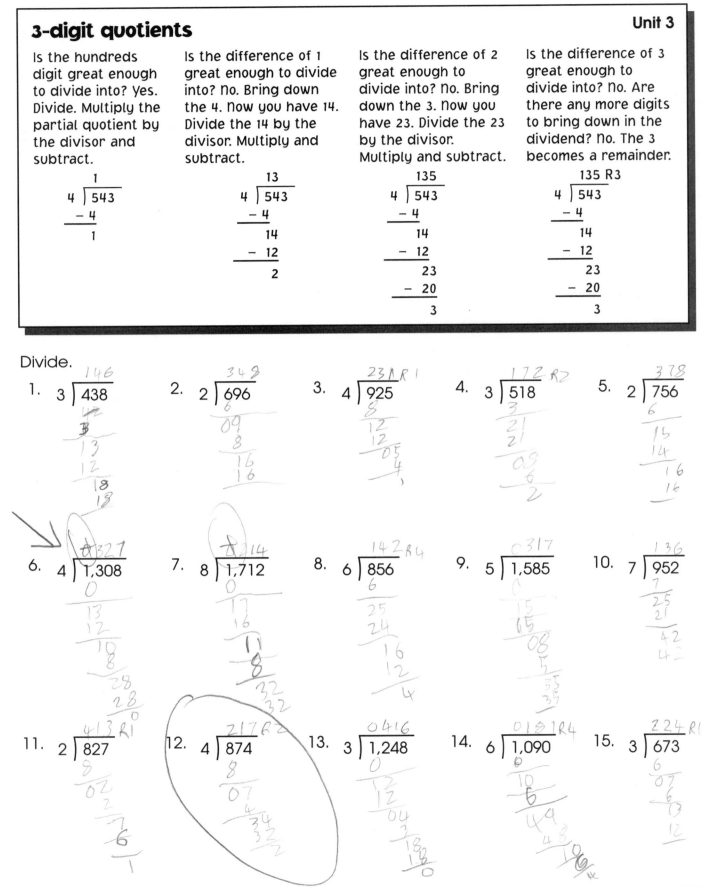

1. 3) 438

2. 2) 696

3. 4) 925

4. 3) 518

5. 2) 756

6. 4) 1,308

7. 8) 1,712

8. 6) 856

9. 5) 1,585

10. 7) 952

11. 2) 827

12. 4) 874

13. 3) 1,248

14. 6) 1,090

15. 3) 673

Teach & Test Math: Grade 5

Zeroes in the quotients

Is the thousands digit great enough to divide into? No. Divide into the 12 hundreds. Divide. Multiply the partial quotient by the divisor and subtract.

$$
\begin{array}{r}
3 \\
4\overline{)1227} \\
-12 \\
\hline
0
\end{array}
$$

Is the difference of 0 great enough to divide into? No. Bring down the 2 tens. Are the 2 tens great enough to divide into? No again! It is still not enough to divide into. <u>Place a zero in the quotient.</u>

$$
\begin{array}{r}
30 \\
4\overline{)1227} \\
-12 \\
\hline
02
\end{array}
$$

Bring down the 7 ones. Are the 27 ones great enough to be divided into? Yes. Multiply the partial quotient by the divisor and subtract.

$$
\begin{array}{r}
306 \\
4\overline{)1227} \\
-12 \\
\hline
027 \\
-24 \\
\hline
3
\end{array}
$$

Is the difference of 3 great enough to divide into? No. Are there any more digits to bring down in the dividend? No. 3 then becomes a remainder.

$$
\begin{array}{r}
306\ \text{R3} \\
4\overline{)1227} \\
-12 \\
\hline
027 \\
-24 \\
\hline
3
\end{array}
$$

Divide.

1. 4)203   50 R3
  20
  03
  0
  9

2. 3)1,206   0402

3. 2)1,620   810

4. 5)545   109

5. 2)961   480 R1

6. 7)725   103 R4

7. 9)278   30 R8

8. 5)1,549   309 R4

9. 3)2,340   750

10. 6)1,235   205 R5

11. 4)363   90 R3

12. 6)650   108 R2

13. 3)2,040   680

14. 6)659   109 R5

15. 4)834   208 R?

16. 7)1,056   150 R6

17. 8)850   106 R2

18. 5)1,035   207

19. 7)2,107   301

20. 9)920   102 R2

Name

Dividing money

Place the dollar sign and the decimal point in the quotient.

$$\begin{array}{r} \$\ \ .\ \ \\ 3\overline{)\,\$12.75} \end{array}$$

Is the digit in the ten dollars place great enough to divide into? No. Divide into 12 dollars. Multiply the partial quotient by the divisor and subtract.

$$\begin{array}{r} \$4.\ \ \ \ \\ 3\overline{)\,\$12.75} \\ -12\ \ \ \\ \hline 0\ \ \ \end{array}$$

Is the difference great enough to divide into? No. Bring down the 7. Divide. Multiply and subtract.

$$\begin{array}{r} \$4.2\ \ \\ 3\overline{)\,\$12.75} \\ -12\ \ \ \\ \hline 07\ \\ -\ 6\ \\ \hline 1\ \end{array}$$

Is the difference great enough to divide into? No. Bring down the 5. Multiply and subtract. Is the 0 great enough to divide into? No. Are there any more digits to bring down? No. You are finished.

$$\begin{array}{r} \$4.25 \\ 3\overline{)\,\$12.75} \\ -12\ \ \ \\ \hline 07\ \\ -\ 6\ \\ \hline 15 \\ -15 \\ \hline 0 \end{array}$$

Divide.

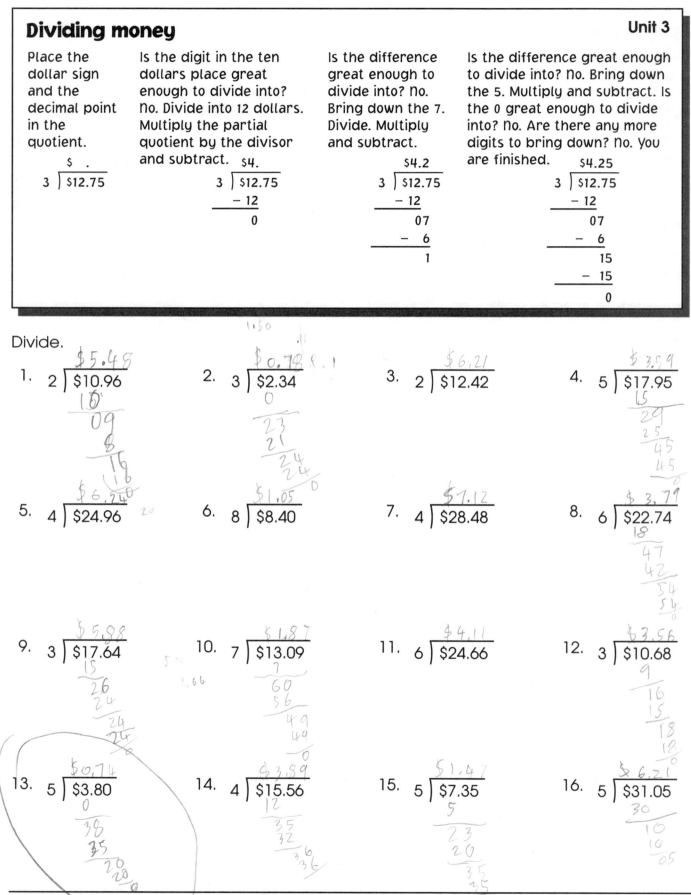

1. $2\overline{)\,\$10.96}$

2. $3\overline{)\,\$2.34}$

3. $2\overline{)\,\$12.42}$

4. $5\overline{)\,\$17.95}$

5. $4\overline{)\,\$24.96}$

6. $8\overline{)\,\$8.40}$

7. $4\overline{)\,\$28.48}$

8. $6\overline{)\,\$22.74}$

9. $3\overline{)\,\$17.64}$

10. $7\overline{)\,\$13.09}$

11. $6\overline{)\,\$24.66}$

12. $3\overline{)\,\$10.68}$

13. $5\overline{)\,\$3.80}$

14. $4\overline{)\,\$15.56}$

15. $5\overline{)\,\$7.35}$

16. $5\overline{)\,\$31.05}$

Estimating the quotients

Unit 3

Round the divisor to the nearest ten.	Estimate how many 40s there are in the first three digits (166). 40 cannot divide into the first digit, 1, or the first two digits, 16, but easily divides into 166.	Multiply and subtract.	Next, begin dividing to find the actual quotient.

$$37\overline{)1{,}665}$$

$$40\overline{)1{,}665}$$

$$\begin{array}{r}4\\40\overline{)1{,}665}\end{array}$$

$$\begin{array}{r}41\\40\overline{)1{,}665}\\-160\\\hline 65\end{array}$$

$$\begin{array}{r}45\\37\overline{)1{,}665}\\-148\\\hline 185\\-185\\\hline 0\end{array}$$

Round each divisor to the nearest 10. Estimate. Then find the actual quotient. See how close your estimate really is!

Estimate   **Actual quotient**   **Estimate**   **Actual quotient**

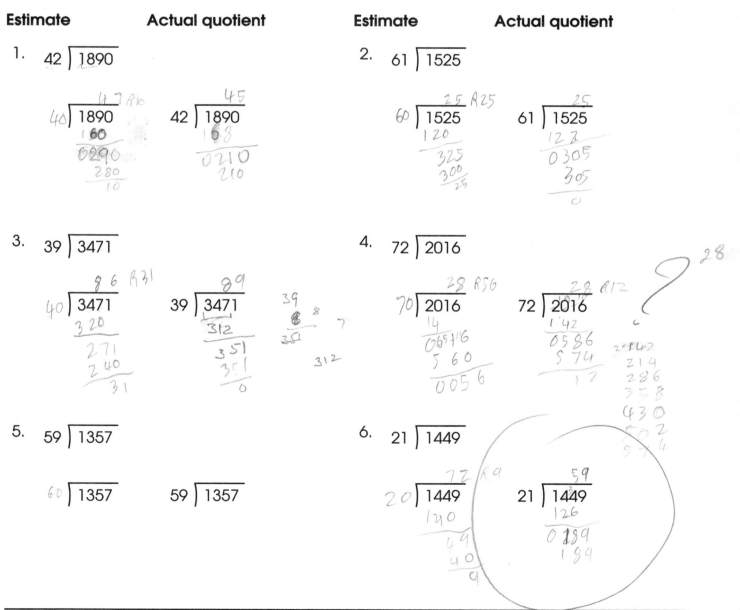

1. $42\overline{)1890}$

2. $61\overline{)1525}$

3. $39\overline{)3471}$

4. $72\overline{)2016}$

5. $59\overline{)1357}$

6. $21\overline{)1449}$

One-digit quotients (two-digit divisors)   **Unit 3**

$$39 \overline{)316}$$

Is the hundreds digit great enough to divide into by 39? No. So, we must divide into the 316 ones!

$$39 \overline{)316} \quad 40 \overline{)316}^{\,7}$$

How many groups of 39 are there in 316? To help estimate, round the divisor 39 to 40. Think: there are eight 40s in 320. That is too many. So, the partial quotient might be 7.

$$\begin{array}{r} 7 \\ 39 \overline{)316} \\ -273 \\ \hline 43 \end{array} \qquad \begin{array}{r} 8 \\ 39 \overline{)316} \\ -312 \\ \hline 4 \end{array}$$

43 > 39   Stop!   4 < 39

Multiply and subtract. Is the difference of 43 less than the divisor? No! The difference in any division problem when you estimate the partial quotient must be less than the divisor. Use 8 as the partial quotient. Multiply and subtract. Is the difference of 4 less than 39? Yes!

$$\begin{array}{r} 8\ R4 \\ 39 \overline{)316} \\ -312 \\ \hline 4 \end{array}$$

Is the difference of 4 great enough to divide into by 39? No. 4 then, becomes the remainder.

Note: estimating allows you to use trial and error to arrive at the exact quotient. It also allows you to get closer to the correct quotient in less time than guessing.

Divide. Note: the remainder can be any digit <u>less than</u> the divisor.

1. $13 \overline{)117}$

2. $46 \overline{)328}$

3. $29 \overline{)181}$

4. $54 \overline{)432}$

5. $61 \overline{)345}$

6. $82 \overline{)378}$

7. $28 \overline{)252}$

8. $19 \overline{)140}$

9. $42 \overline{)346}$

10. $38 \overline{)151}$

11. $21 \overline{)126}$

12. $48 \overline{)462}$

13. $71 \overline{)430}$

14. $80 \overline{)799}$

15. $51 \overline{)255}$

Write two problems with two-digit divisors that have the same remainders.

Two-digit quotients (two-digit divisors)   Unit 3

Is the thousands digit great enough to divide into by 24? No. How about 13 hundreds? No. So, we must divide into the 136 tens!

```
24 ) 1367
```

How many groups of 24 are there in 136? Think: there are 5 groups of 25 in 125. So, let's try 5 as our partial quotient. Multiply and subtract.

```
       5
24 ) 1367
   - 120
      16
```

Is the difference great enough to be divided into by 24? No. Bring down the 7. How many groups of 24 are there in 167? Multiply and subtract.

```
      56
24 ) 1367
   - 120
      167
   - 144
       23
```

Is the difference of 23 great enough to divide into by 24? No. It is less than the divisor. It becomes the remainder.

```
      56 R23
24 ) 1367
   - 120
      167
   - 144
       23
```

Divide.

1.
```
      4 3
16 ) 688
     64
     48
     48
      0
```

2.
```
      56 R6
32 ) 1,798
     160
     198
     192
       6
```

3. 21) 629

4. 41) 1,596

5. 81) 1,155

6. 42) 1,512

7. 51) 1,468

8. 72) 1,562

9. 14) 518

10. 22) 792

11. 19) 1,652

12. 31) 490

13. 49) 3,078

Three-digit quotients (two-digit divisors) — Unit 3

Is the 2 in the thousands place great enough to divide into by 21? No. So, we divide into the 26 hundreds! Multiply and subtract.

```
        1
21 ) 2699
   - 21
      5
```

Is the difference of 5 great enough to be divided into by 21? No. Bring down the 9. Divide. Multiply and subtract.

```
       12
21 ) 2699
   - 21
      59
   - 42
      17
```

Is the difference of 17 great enough to be divided into by 21? No. Bring down the 9. Divide. Multiply and subtract.

```
      128
21 ) 2699
   - 21
      59
   - 42
     179
   - 168
      11
```

Is the difference of 11 great enough to divide into by 21? No. It is less than the divisor. It becomes the remainder.

```
     128 R11
21 ) 2699
   - 21
      59
   - 42
     179
   - 168
      11
```

Divide.

1. 21) 6,559

2. 40) 5,099

3. 51) 7,864

4. 16) 6,607

5. 31) 4,371

6. 71) 8,073

7. 18) 2,568

8. 69) 7,916

9. 32) 6,900

10. 59) 7,374

11. 15) 3,270

12. 22) 6,928

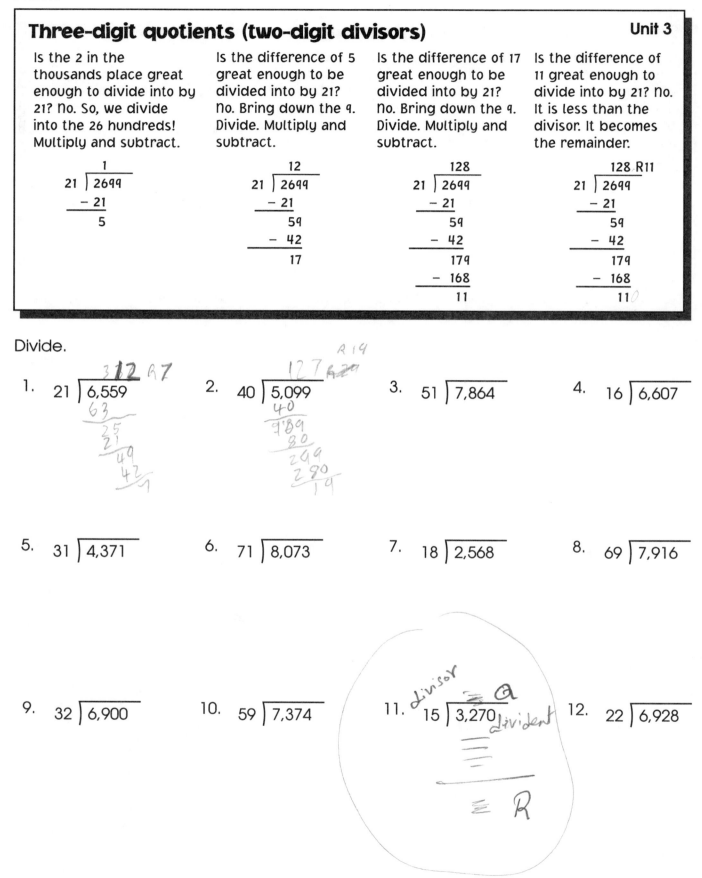

Name

Read the question. Use an extra piece of paper
to write problems down and solve them.
Fill in the circle beside the best answer.

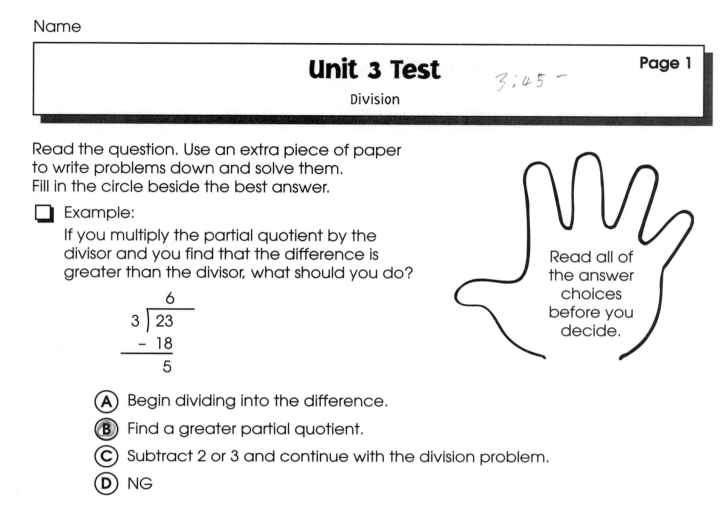

📖 Example:

If you multiply the partial quotient by the
divisor and you find that the difference is
greater than the divisor, what should you do?

$$
\begin{array}{r}
6 \\
3\overline{)23} \\
-18 \\
\hline
5
\end{array}
$$

Read all of
the answer
choices
before you
decide.

Ⓐ Begin dividing into the difference.

Ⓑ Find a greater partial quotient.

Ⓒ Subtract 2 or 3 and continue with the division problem.

Ⓓ NG

Answer: B because the difference
must be less than the divisor.

Now try these. You have 20 minutes. Continue until you see ⬡STOP .

1. $7\overline{)30}$	5 Ⓐ	3 R9 Ⓑ	4 R2 Ⓒ	2 R4 Ⓓ
2. $6\overline{)34}$	5 R4 Ⓐ	4 R10 Ⓑ	6 R2 Ⓒ	4 R5 Ⓓ
3. $7\overline{)168}$	20 Ⓐ	24 Ⓑ	26 Ⓒ	NG Ⓓ

GO ON

4.

$$4 \overline{)147}$$

35 R8 (A) 17 R7 (B) 36 R3 (C) 33 R6 (D)

5. Where is the mistake in this problem?

$$7 \overline{)165} \quad 23\,R1$$
$$\underline{-14}$$
$$25$$
$$\underline{-24}$$
$$1$$

(A) 7 x 2 does not equal 14.

(B) The remainder should be 0.

(C) 7 x 3 does not equal 24.

(D) NG

6. Why should this problem be redone?

$$4 \overline{)103} \quad 1$$
$$\underline{-4}$$
$$6$$

(A) 4 x 1 does not equal 4.

(B) 10 minus 4 does not equal 6.

(C) The difference (6) is greater than the divisor (4).

(D) NG

7.

$$3 \overline{)470}$$

156 R9 (A) 138 R4 (B) 156 R5 (C) NG (D)

8.

$$5 \overline{)1,170}$$

234 (A) 264 R2 (B) 251 R5 (C) 234 R2 (D)

9. The zero is in what place value in the quotient?

$$5 \overline{)530} \quad 106$$

thousands (A) hundreds (B) ones (C) tens (D)

10.

$$6 \overline{)1,233}$$

350 R2 (A) 250 R8 (B) 205 R3 (C) 203 R5 (D)

GO ON

11. What is wrong with this problem?

```
       3.27
  5 ) $16.35
    - 15
      13
     - 10
        35
      - 35
         0
```

(A) There is a subtraction mistake.

(B) The dollar sign is missing.

(C) There is a multiplication mistake.

(D) NG

12.

```
  6 ) $8.70
```

$1.45
(A)

$3.12
(B)

$1.89
(C)

$1.54
(D)

13. Estimate the quotient.

```
  42 ) 882
```

35
(A)

42
(B)

21
(C)

25
(D)

14. When estimating, what is a good number to round in a division problem?

the product
(A)

the quotient
(B)

the divisor
(C)

the difference
(D)

15. When dividing, the difference must always be less than the:

divisor
(A)

sum
(B)

product
(C)

quotient
(D)

16.

```
  28 ) 170
```

6 R2
(A)

7 R8
(B)

5 R25
(C)

5 R15
(D)

GO ON ⟶

Unit 3 Test

17. What would you round the divisor to in estimating this quotient?

$$39 \overline{)312}$$

30	35	40	39
(A)	(B)	(C)	(D)

18.

$$15 \overline{)395}$$

15 R10	26 R5	30 R10	28 R5
(A)	(B)	(C)	(D)

19. Where is the mistake in this problem?

$$
\begin{array}{r}
15 \text{ R19} \\
23 \overline{)365} \\
-\ 23 \\
\hline
135 \\
-\ 115 \\
\hline
20
\end{array}
$$

(A) The subtraction is incorrect.

(B) The multiplication is incorrect.

(C) There should be 3 digits in the quotient.

(D) NG

20.

$$15 \overline{)1,845}$$

123	321	403	NG
(A)	(B)	(C)	(D)

Why is it important to know when to place a zero in the quotient?

You might get the answer mixed up.

If the zero is misplaced or left out, will that change the answer? How?

Yes

misplaced the zero here and get it wrong

STOP

Tenths   Unit 4

ones	tenths
2 .	4

$2\frac{4}{10}$

What portion of these boxes are shaded? each entire box

What portion of this box is shaded? four tenths of the box

Altogether equals: 2.4 (two and four tenths)

This can be spoken, "two point four," or "two and four tenths."

Note: When writing a decimal, if there are no whole numbers, place a zero left of the decimal point. Examples: seven tenths = 0.7, nine tenths = 0.9

Write the decimal.

1. three and five tenths _____

2. six and one tenth _____

3. eight tenths _____

4. eight and three tenths _____

5. three tenths _____

6. two and one tenth _____

7. seven tenths _____

8. twenty and two tenths _____

9. four tenths _____

10. thirty-seven and two tenths _____

11. four hundred and one tenth _____

12. fifty-five and three tenths _____

13. six tenths _____

14. one tenth _____

Write the word name for each decimal. Example: 5.6 = five and six tenths

15. 3.9 _____

16. 2.7 _____

17. 12.8 _____

18. 7.3 _____

Write the fraction or mixed number that represents each decimal.

19. 0.6 _____

20. 0.5 _____

21. 0.9 _____

22. 0.7 _____

23. 1.2 _____

24. 4.8 _____

25. 6.1 _____

26. 3.4 _____

27. 33.2 _____

28. 21.8 _____

Hundredths

ones		tenths	hundredths
1	.	3	2

$1 \frac{32}{100}$

What portion of this box is shaded?
The entire box.

What portion of this box is shaded?
32 hundredths of the box

Altogether the total shaded area equals: 1.32
(one and thirty-two hundredths)
This can be spoken, "one point thirty-two", or "one and thirty-two hundredths."

Match each decimal to its word name. Use a ruler to connect the dots.

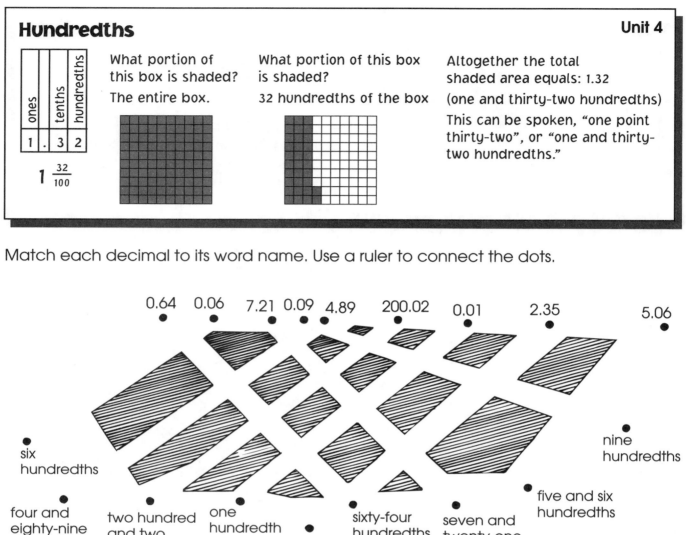

0.64   0.06   7.21   0.09   4.89   200.02   0.01   2.35   5.06

six hundredths

nine hundredths

four and eighty-nine hundredths

two hundred and two hundredths

one hundredth

two and thirty-five hundredths

sixty-four hundredths

seven and twenty-one hundredths

five and six hundredths

Write the fraction or mixed number that represents each decimal.

1. 0.08 _____

2. 6.09 _____

3. 2.12 _____

4. 0.21 _____

5. 7.34 _____

6. 0.55 _____

7. 16.08 _____

8. 300.24 _____

9. 25.04 _____

10. 600.49 _____

11. 0.72 _____

12. 0.22 _____

Thousandths

ones	tenths	hundredths	thousandths
0	.5	2	7

0.527 is spoken as, "five hundred twenty-seven thousandths."

fraction: $\frac{527}{1000}$

Unit 4

Write the decimal.

1. three hundred and seven hundredths _____

2. fifteen and forty-five thousandths _____

3. two hundred eighteen and four thousandths _____

4. two thousandths _____

5. sixty-seven and six hundred thirty-one thousandths _____

6. twelve thousandths _____

7. forty-nine and ninety-nine thousandths _____

8. five and eight hundred forty-five thousandths _____

9. eight thousandths _____

10. ten and six hundred two thousandths _____

11. three thousandths _____

"FIVE HUNDRED TWENTY-SEVEN THOUSANDTHS"

0.527

Write the decimal's word name.

12. 0.035 _____

13. 89.004 _____

14. 324.008 _____

15. 72.045 _____

Write the fraction or mixed number that represents each decimal.

16. 3.047 _____   17. 289.078 _____   18. 73.034 _____   19. 556.345 _____

20. 3.657 _____   21. 900.002 _____   22. 0.5_____   23. 4.8_____

Comparing and ordering decimals

8.009 > 8.005

When comparing decimals, always begin with the greatest digit on the left-hand side. Then move to the right, comparing each set of digits. A number line clearly shows which decimal has a greater value.

5.15 < 5.35   or   5.35 > 5.15

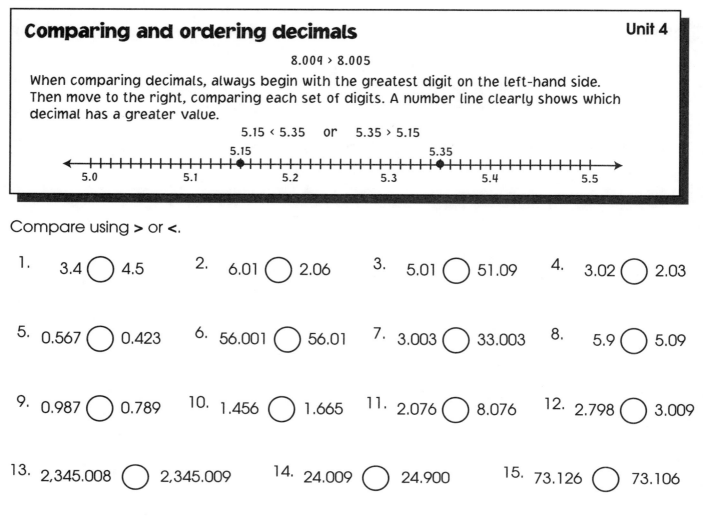

Compare using > or <.

1. 3.4 ◯ 4.5

2. 6.01 ◯ 2.06

3. 5.01 ◯ 51.09

4. 3.02 ◯ 2.03

5. 0.567 ◯ 0.423

6. 56.001 ◯ 56.01

7. 3.003 ◯ 33.003

8. 5.9 ◯ 5.09

9. 0.987 ◯ 0.789

10. 1.456 ◯ 1.665

11. 2.076 ◯ 8.076

12. 2.798 ◯ 3.009

13. 2,345.008 ◯ 2,345.009

14. 24.009 ◯ 24.900

15. 73.126 ◯ 73.106

List the decimals on the number lines. Then order from least to greatest.

_____ _____ _____ _____ _____ _____ _____

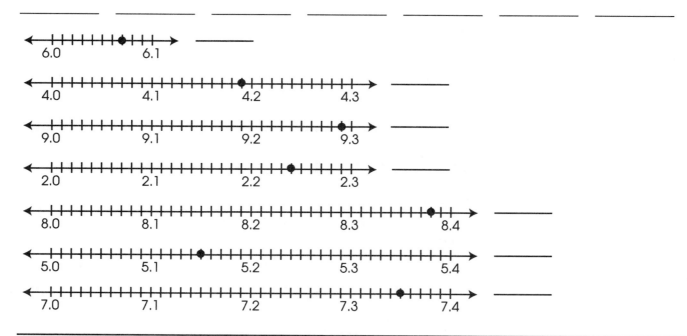

Rounding decimals

Remember the rule: "If it's 4 or less, round down. If it's 5 or more, round up!"

When rounding to the nearest whole number:

3.2134 = 3

Look at the digit in the tenths place. (It is 4 or less (2), so we round down!)

When rounding to the nearest tenth:

45.289 = 45.3

Look at the digit in the hundredths place. (It is 5 or more (8), so we round up!)

When rounding to the nearest hundredth:

22.345 = 22.35

Look at the digit in the thousandths place. (It is 5 or more (8), so we round up!)

Round to the nearest whole number.

1. 45.678 _____   2.68 _____   612.123 _____   89.519 _____

2. 2,345.5 _____   7.29 _____   1.398 _____   4.916 _____

3. 87.056 _____   43.089 _____   234.768 _____   0.897 _____

4. 567.289 _____   7.8 _____   6.29 _____   95.032 _____

Round to the nearest tenth.

5. 4.379 _____   2.819 _____   543.18 _____   0.54 _____

6. 56.14 _____   3.157 _____   78.028 _____   678.456 _____

7. 0.417 _____   36.192 _____   1.248 _____   0.25 _____

8. 34.248 _____   8.77 _____   16.651 _____   8.991 _____

Round to the nearest hundredth.

9. 34.248 _____   5.251 _____   6.108 _____   45.814 _____

10. 5.213 _____   9.178 _____   23.682 _____   38.199 _____

11. 2.454 _____   9.017 _____   7.271 _____   435.458 _____

12. 6.319 _____   2,345.124 _____   6.237 _____   45.835 _____

Name

Adding decimals   Unit 4

Make sure all decimal points are lined up.	Place a decimal point in the sum.	Add.
6.142 7.2 + 0.143	6.142 7.2 + 0.143 .	6.142 7.2 + 0.143 13.485

Add. Line up all the decimal points before you begin.

1. 3.2 + 21.14 + 321.9   2. 6.416 + 25.3   3. 14.6 + 0.3 + 1.257

4. 7 + 0.34 + 1.215   5. 0.34 + 0.2 + 0.121   6. 86 + 0.2 + 1.3

7. 49.1 + 0.84 + 1.3   8. 23.7 + 0.416   9. 0.2 + 1.5 + 0.8

10. 4.2 + 1.6 + 0.313   11. 9.2 + 24.36 + 0.14   12. 5.2 + 0.4 + 1.34

Add.

13.
```
      6.
      3.2
  +   0.45
```

14.
```
      3.145
      0.2
  +  15.9
```

15.
```
      8.462
  +  23.89
```

16.
```
      7.
      6.43
  +  12.125
```

17.
```
     24.5
      0.9
  +   1.238
```

18.
```
      0.6
     12.3
  +   0.14
```

19.
```
     76.4
      3.516
  +   0.318
```

20.
```
      0.814
     21.3
  +   3.14
```

Subtracting decimals

Unit 4

When subtracting a decimal from a whole number, add a decimal point and as many zeros as there are digits behind the decimal point.

```
  6.000
- 2.145
```

Place a decimal point in the sum.

```
  6.000
- 2.145
.
```

Subtract.

```
       9  9
    5 10 10 10
    6̶.0̶0̶0̶
  - 2.1 4 5
    3.8 5 5
```

Subtract. Complete the cross-number puzzle.

Across:

1.
```
    8
-  2.9
```

3.
```
  46.3
- 3.24
```

5.
```
   5.8
-  2.9
```

7.
```
  35.96
- 2.328
```

9.
```
  35.42
- 21.28
```

11.
```
   7.6
-  2.8
```

13.
```
  68.4
- 2.32
```

14.
```
   12
-  2.8
```

15.
```
   5.6
- 0.38
```

18.
```
   9.6
- 2.35
```

Down:

2.
```
    3
- 1.341
```

3.
```
   65
- 21.35
```

4.
```
  3.46
- 2.126
```

5.
```
   3.45
- 1.232
```

6.
```
  64.8
- 2.317
```

8.
```
    7
- 5.35
```

10.
```
  3.8
- 1.9
```

12.
```
  89.42
- 3.5
```

16.
```
  34.4
- 12.9
```

17.
```
   6.2
- 3.5
```

Estimating decimals   Unit 4

To estimate the sum, round each   Add.
decimal to its greatest place value.

34.619	30		30
+ 81.54	+ 80		+ 80
			110

To estimate the difference, round each   Subtract.
decimal to its greatest place value.

87.912	90		90
− 21.345	− 20		− 20
			70

Estimate the sum. Round to the greatest place value.

1.
2.34 →
+ 8.95 → + _____

2.
649.200 →
+ 87.425 → + _____

3.
0.315 →
+ 0.492 → + _____

4.
67.45 →
+ 89.21 → + _____

5.
789.4 →
+ 325.89 → + _____

6.
32.8 →
+ 121.4 → + _____

Estimate the difference. Round to the greatest place value.

7.
462.5 →
− 291.8 → − _____

8.
2,498.6 →
− 1,149.8 → − _____

9.
582.65 →
− 216.95 → − _____

10.
0.924 →
− 0.287 → − _____

11.
6,841.79 →
− 2,145.62 → − _____

12.
634.482 →
− 395.346 → − _____

Multiplying decimals   Unit 4

Multiply decimals like you do as a regular number. But, when you are done, count the number of digits behind the decimal points in the problem.

Make sure that the product has an equal number of digits behind the decimal point.

```
    2.5
  x 3.4
  ------
    100
    750
  ------
    850
```

```
    2.5   1 digit behind the decimal point
  x 3.4   1 digit behind the decimal point
  ------
    100
    750
  ------
   8.50   2 digits behind the decimal point
```

Multiply.

1.
```
    815
  x 7.3
```

2.
```
    0.7
  x 0.8
```

3.
```
   3.05
  x  0.4
```

4.
```
   2.15
  x  0.5
```

5.
```
    3.4
  x 5.9
```

6.
```
    3.9
  x 0.4
```

7.
```
    7.6
  x 8.9
```

8.
```
    0.4
  x 2.8
```

9.
```
   1.23
  x   39
```

10.
```
  153.4
  x  0.2
```

11.
```
   0.03
  x  0.6
```

12.
```
    8.2
  x 1.4
```

13.
```
    3.6
  x 2.4
```

14.
```
   5.02
  x  0.3
```

15.
```
    0.6
  x 2.9
```

16.
```
    5.6
  x 3.8
```

17.
```
  34.05
  x    7
```

18.
```
   3.12
  x  0.9
```

19.
```
    5.6
  x 0.9
```

20.
```
  81.23
  x  0.4
```

Dividing decimals

$8 \overline{)1.5}$

It may be necessary to add zeros to the dividend when you divide. You can add as many as you need. Add them one at a time, as needed.

```
      0.1
  8 ) 1.5
    - 8
      7
```

```
      0.18
  8 ) 1.50
    - 8
      70
    - 64
      6
```

```
      0.187
  8 ) 1.500
    - 8
      70
    - 64
      60
    - 56
      4
```

```
      0.1875
  8 ) 1.5000
    - 8
      70
    - 64
      60
    - 56
      40
    - 40
      0
```

Divide.

1. $5 \overline{)0.10}$

2. $9 \overline{)0.72}$

3. $42 \overline{)1.26}$

4. $12 \overline{)0.84}$

5. $21 \overline{)6.3}$

6. $48 \overline{)1.92}$

7. $56 \overline{)151.2}$

8. $29 \overline{)4.06}$

9. $61 \overline{)88.45}$

10. $16 \overline{)39.52}$

11. $8 \overline{)28.48}$

12. $5 \overline{)9.45}$

13. $14 \overline{)36.12}$

14. $22 \overline{)74.8}$

15. $7 \overline{)29.82}$

16. $19 \overline{)5.13}$

Name

Read the question. Use an extra piece of paper to write problems down and solve them.
Fill in the circle beside the best answer.

☐ Example:
What is the correct answer?

```
    1.25
  x    5
  ─────────
    625
```

62.5   0.625   -6.25   NG
(A)   (B)   (C)   (D)

If you are not sure what the answer is, skip it and come back to it later.

Answer: C because the number of digits behind the decimal point in the problem should be the same amount that are in the answer.

Now try these. You have 20 minutes. Continue until you see ⬡STOP.

---

1. Write $\frac{8}{10}$ as a decimal.

8.0   0.8   80   0.08
(A)   (B)   (C)   (D)

---

2. Match the decimal for thirty and two tenths.

0.32   32.10   320   30.2
(A)   (B)   (C)   (D)

---

3. Match the decimal for seven and twenty-four hundredths.

7.24   0.724   72.4   NG
(A)   (B)   (C)   (D)

---

4. What is the word name for 6.03?

(A) sixty-three hundredths   (B) six and zero three

(C) six and three hundredths   (D) six and three tenths

GO ON ⟩

Unit 4 Test

5. Which decimal matches this fraction?

$6\frac{125}{1000}$

6.6125
(A)

60.125
(B)

6.125
(C)

61.25
(D)

6. Match the fraction for 21.047.

$21\frac{047}{100}$
(A)

$21\frac{47}{1000}$
(B)

$\frac{21047}{1000}$
(C)

NG
(D)

7. Order the following decimals from least to greatest: 0.04, 0.4, 0.004, 4.04

(A) 4.04, 0.4, 0.04, 0.004

(B) 0.004, 0.4, 4.04, 0.04

(C) 0.004, 0.04, 0.4, 4.04

(D) 0.4, 0.04, 0.004, 4.04

8. Compare using >, <, or =.

5.005 ◯ 5.05

>
(A)

<
(B)

=
(C)

NG
(D)

9. Round 0.863 to the greatest place value.

0.800
(A)

0.86
(B)

0.9
(C)

0.7
(D)

10. Round 64.249 to the nearest hundredth.

64.25
(A)

64.2
(B)

64.30
(C)

64
(D)

11. Add.

$3.41 + 0.6 + 1.2$

4.89
(A)

6.24
(B)

5.21
(C)

4.49
(D)

12. Which problem is written correctly?

$$\begin{array}{r} 312.4 \\ +\ \ 2.158 \\ \hline \end{array}$$

(A)

$$\begin{array}{r} 312.4 \\ +\quad 2.158 \\ \hline \end{array}$$

(B)

$$\begin{array}{r} 312.4 \\ +\quad 2.158 \\ \hline \end{array}$$

(C)

NG

(D)

13.

$$\begin{array}{r} 62.41 \\ 0.23 \\ +\ \ 1.8 \\ \hline 64.44 \end{array}$$

644.4 (A)   60.89 (B)   68.51 (C)   64.44 (D)

14. How many zeros need to be added to this problem as you subtract?

$$\begin{array}{r} 3. \\ -\ 1.689 \\ \hline \end{array}$$

none (A)   3 (B)   2 (C)   1 (D)

15.

$$\begin{array}{r} 2 \\ -\ 1.346 \\ \hline \end{array}$$

0.654 (A)   1.346 (B)   1.764 (C)   3.346 (D)

16.

$$\begin{array}{r} 72.495 \\ -\ 1.362 \\ \hline \end{array}$$

71.894 (A)   71.133 (B)   7.235 (C)   73.857 (D)

17.

$$\begin{array}{r} 23.41 \\ \times\quad 0.8 \\ \hline 18.728 \end{array}$$

19.842 (A)   18.72 (B)   1.872 (C)   NG (D)

GO ON

Unit 4 Test

18.

31.24
x   7.2

| 2,249.28 (A) | 224.928 (B) | 22,492.8 (C) | 22.4928 (D) |

19.

6) 17.34

| 2.89 (A) | 3.46 (B) | 3.87 (C) | NG (D) |

20.

3) 0.15

| 0.05 (A) | 0.5 (B) | 05.0 (C) | 0.005 (D) |

I have $10. I want to buy a bag of apples for $3.92 and a sack of potatoes for $4.95. Why is it good to estimate the sum before I get to the register to pay for them?

To see if you have enough money.

When would it be important to know the exact amount when buying more than one item?

To make sure you have enough money. When we are ready to pay

STOP

Midway Review Test Name Grid

Write your name in pencil in the boxes along the top. Begin with your last name. Fill in as many letters as will fit. Then follow the columns straight down and bubble in the letters that correspond with the letters in your name. Complete the rest of the information the same way. You may use a piece of scrap paper to help you keep your place.

STUDENT'S NAME																			SCHOOL
LAST											FIRST							MI	TEACHER

FEMALE ○   MALE ○

DATE OF BIRTH

MONTH	DAY	YEAR
JAN ○	⓪ ⓪	⓪ ⓪
FEB ○	① ①	① ①
MAR ○	② ②	② ②
APR ○	③ ③	③ ③
MAY ○	④	④ ④
JUN ○	⑤	⑤ ⑤
JUL ○	⑥	⑥ ⑥
AUG ○	⑦	⑦ ⑦
SEP ⊛	⑧	⑧ ⑧
OCT ○	⑨	⑨ ⑨
NOV ○		
DEC ○		

GRADE ③   ④   ⑤

(Name grid columns with bubbles A–Z for each letter position)

Midway Review Test Answer Sheet

Pay close attention when transferring your answers. Fill in the bubbles neatly and completely. You may use a piece of scrap paper to help you keep your place.

SAMPLES
A Ⓐ Ⓑ ● Ⓓ
B Ⓕ ● Ⓗ Ⓙ

1 Ⓐ Ⓑ Ⓒ Ⓓ
2 Ⓕ Ⓖ Ⓗ Ⓙ
3 Ⓐ Ⓑ Ⓒ Ⓓ
4 Ⓕ Ⓖ Ⓗ Ⓙ
5 Ⓐ Ⓑ Ⓒ Ⓓ
6 Ⓕ Ⓖ Ⓗ Ⓙ

7 Ⓐ Ⓑ Ⓒ Ⓓ
8 Ⓕ Ⓖ Ⓗ Ⓙ
9 Ⓐ Ⓑ Ⓒ Ⓓ
10 Ⓕ Ⓖ Ⓗ Ⓙ
11 Ⓐ Ⓑ Ⓒ Ⓓ
12 Ⓕ Ⓖ Ⓗ Ⓙ

13 Ⓐ Ⓑ Ⓒ Ⓓ
14 Ⓕ Ⓖ Ⓗ Ⓙ
15 Ⓐ Ⓑ Ⓒ Ⓓ
16 Ⓕ Ⓖ Ⓗ Ⓙ
17 Ⓐ Ⓑ Ⓒ Ⓓ
18 Ⓕ Ⓖ Ⓗ Ⓙ

19 Ⓐ Ⓑ Ⓒ Ⓓ
20 Ⓕ Ⓖ Ⓗ Ⓙ
21 Ⓐ Ⓑ Ⓒ Ⓓ
22 Ⓕ Ⓖ Ⓗ Ⓙ
23 Ⓐ Ⓑ Ⓒ Ⓓ
24 Ⓕ Ⓖ Ⓗ Ⓙ

25 Ⓐ Ⓑ Ⓒ Ⓓ

Midway Review Test

Read the question. Use an extra piece of paper to write problems down and solve them. Fill in the circle beside the best answer.

☐ Example:

What is the value of the underlined digit?

3,123,5̲46,789

(A) five hundred

(B) five hundred thousand

(C) five million

(D) NG

Answer: B

Now try these. You have 25 minutes.

Continue until you see ⬡STOP.

Remember your Helping Hand Strategies:

1. Sometimes the correct answer is not given. Fill in the circle beside NG if no answer is correct.

2. Always read each question carefully.

3. Read all the answer choices before you decide.

4. If you are not sure what the answer is, skip it and come back to it later.

6:43 -

---

1. What is the value of the underlined digit? 641̲,348,389

one thousand	one billion	one million	one hundred
(A)	(B)	(C) ●	(D)

---

2. When rounding, look to the right of the place value you are rounding to and if:

(F) more than 8, round down.

(G) it is an even number, do not round.

(H) ● 5 or more round up, 4 or less, round down.

(J) NG

---

3. Order the following numbers correctly from least to greatest:

3,062; 362; 306,302; 3,602,362

(A) ● 362; 3,062; 306,302; 3,602,362

(B) 362; 3,602,362; 3,062; 306,302

(C) 3,602,362; 306,302; 3,062; 362

(D) 362; 3,062; 3,602,362; 306,302

GO ON ▷

Midway Review Test

4.

$$\begin{array}{r} {}^{5\ 13} \\ 63,397 \\ -\ 18,075 \\ \hline 45,322 \end{array}$$

81,472   (F)   45,222   (G)   80,072   (H)   45,322   (J)

5. Add. Find the missing digits.

$$\begin{array}{r} 6\square8,143 \\ +133,\square5\square \\ \hline 761,895 \end{array}$$

3, 8, 1   (A)   2, 7, 2   (B)   5, 3, 6   (C)   283   (D)

6.

$$\begin{array}{r} 2,005 \\ -\ 1,783 \end{array}$$

1,085   (F)   222   (G)   1,782   (H)   NG   (J)

7.

$$\begin{array}{r} {}^{1\ 10} \\ \$62.09 \\ -\ 31.82 \\ \hline 3027 \end{array}$$

$30.27   (A) $41.87   (B) $58.42   (C)   NG   (D)

8. Find the value of n. $(5 \times 2) + (5 \times 3) = n \times (2 + 3)$

2   (F)   3   (G)   5   (H)   NG   (J)

9.

$$\begin{array}{r} 2,182 \\ \times\ \ \ \ 3 \end{array}$$

6,346   (A)   6,546   (B)   5,142   (C)   6,664   (D)

10.

$$\begin{array}{r} 38 \\ \times\ \ 24 \end{array}$$

632   (F)   915   (G)   499   (H)   912   (J)

GO ON

11.

$ .23
x   31

$7.13 (A) $6.64 (B) $5.48 (C) $9.20 (D)

12.

$1.35
x   27

$24.99 (F) $27.35 (G) $36.45 (H) $12.05 (J)

13.

603
x   15

9,045 (A)   9,365 (B)   8,045 (C)   NG (D)

14.

6) 23

4 (F)   3 R5 (G)   3 R9 (H)   3 (J)

15.

4) 210

52 R2 (A)   51 (B)   53 R6 (C)   52 (D)

16.

6) 749

149 R3 (F)   625 R2 (G)   124 R5 (H)   NG (J)

17.

5) 1044

200 R5 (A)   208 R4 (B)   201 R44 (C)   207 R6 (D)

18.

$2.58
3) $7.74
6
17
15
24
24

$2.74 (F) $2.58 (G) $3.39 (H) $2.85 (J)

GO ON

19.

21 ⟌ 766

24 R19 Ⓐ   37 R6 Ⓑ   36 R20 Ⓒ   NG Ⓓ

---

20. Write the decimal.

four hundred and three hundred eighty-nine thousandths

400.89 Ⓕ   400.389 Ⓖ   400.3089 Ⓗ   4.389 Ⓙ

---

21. Compare using >, <, or =.

3.042 ◯ 30.423

> Ⓐ   < Ⓑ   = Ⓒ   NG Ⓓ

---

22. Round to the greatest place value.

0.924

1 Ⓕ   0.24 Ⓖ   0.9 Ⓗ   0. Ⓙ

23.

6
2.146
+ 1.39

9.356 Ⓐ   9.256 Ⓑ   9.348 Ⓒ   9.536 Ⓓ

24.

6.004
− 0.382

5.622 Ⓕ   6.002 Ⓖ   3.422 Ⓗ   6.386 Ⓙ

25.

8 ⟌ 3.6

0.45 Ⓐ   2.9 Ⓑ   24.8 Ⓒ   1.45 Ⓓ

Midway Review Test

When estimating decimals, what is the first thing you should do to help you arrive at an approximate answer?

Round to the highest place value.

How does estimating help you?

It helps you know if your answer right.

Line segments, lines, rays, and planes   Unit 5

The straight path between points A and B is a **line segment**. (segment AB)

A **line** is a straight path that goes unending in two directions. (line CD)

A **ray** is a straight path that begins at a point and goes unending in one direction. (ray FG)

A ●———————● B   ←● C   ● D→   ● F   ● G →

Lines that never meet are called **parallel lines**.

Lines that cross are called **intersecting lines**.

Lines that cross at right angles are called **perpendicular lines**.

A flat surface that extends out unending in all directions is a **plane**. (plane D)

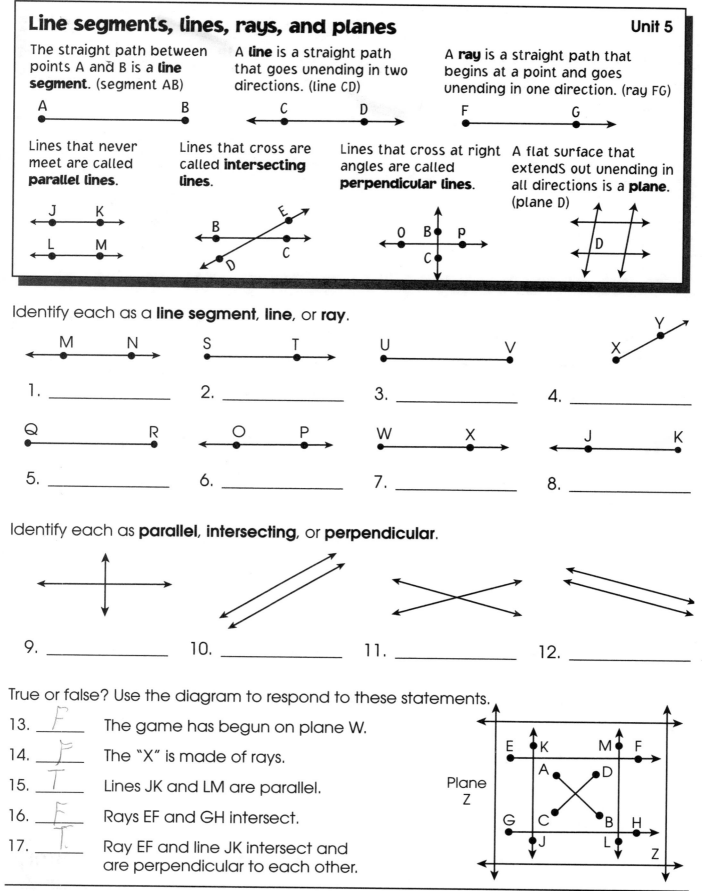

Identify each as a **line segment**, **line**, or **ray**.

M   N   S   T   U   V   X Y

1. _____   2. _____   3. _____   4. _____

Q   R   O   P   W   X   J   K

5. _____   6. _____   7. _____   8. _____

Identify each as **parallel**, **intersecting**, or **perpendicular**.

9. _____   10. _____   11. _____   12. _____

True or false? Use the diagram to respond to these statements.

13. __F__   The game has begun on plane W.

14. __F__   The "X" is made of rays.

15. __T__   Lines JK and LM are parallel.

16. __F__   Rays EF and GH intersect.

17. __T__   Ray EF and line JK intersect and are perpendicular to each other.

Plane Z

Name

Measurement of angles

When two rays share the same end point called the vertex, they create an angle. The degree of the angle can be measured by using a protractor.

Let one ray be the 0° setting, and find the degree of measurement by using the protractor to see where the other ray stands on the protractor.

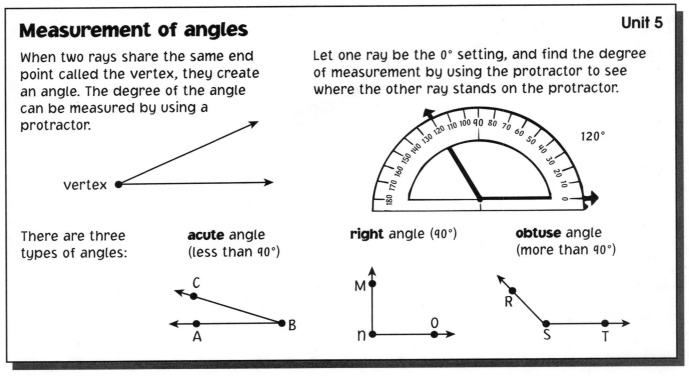

There are three types of angles:

acute angle (less than 90°)

right angle (90°)

obtuse angle (more than 90°)

Find the measurements. Identify as either **acute**, **right**, or **obtuse** angles.

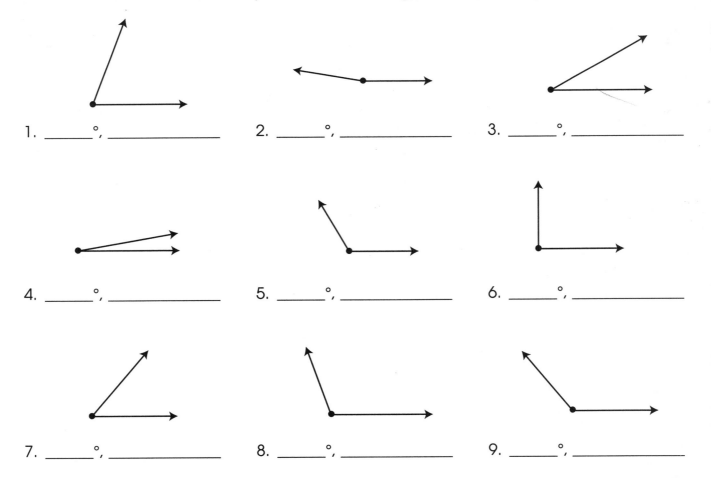

1. _____°, _____

2. _____°, _____

3. _____°, _____

4. _____°, _____

5. _____°, _____

6. _____°, _____

7. _____°, _____

8. _____°, _____

9. _____°, _____

Name _____

Points on a grid

Unit 5

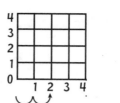

A **grid** contains many points. These points are found by using ordered pairs of numbers such as (2, 4). These numbers, or coordinates, let you know exactly where the point is you are looking for.

The first number of the ordered pair is 2. So, from 0, go over 2.

The second number of the ordered pair is 4. Then go up 4. You have reached the point on the grid!

Make the letter that begins one of the most fun subjects in school! Make each point on the grid using the ordered pairs. As you place them on the grid, draw a line to each new point. At the end, connect that final point to the first one you placed on the grid.

1. (1, 0)   2. (1, 5)   3. (3, 5)   4. (4, 4)   5. (5, 5)

6. (7, 5)   7. (7, 0)   8. (5, 0)   9. (5, 3)   10. (4, 2)

11. (3, 3)   12. (3, 0)   13. (1, 0)

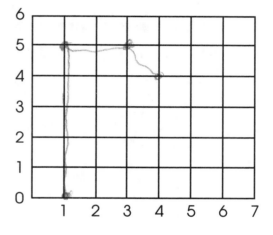

There's a message here for you to read! Write the letters for each ordered pair.

M   A   I   H   I   S   O   N   E
(2, 1) (4, 5) (1, 3) (8, 3)   (1, 0) (4, 1)   (5, 4) (7, 1) (1, 5)   (5, 4) (4, 3)   (1, 3) (8, 3) (1, 5)

(1, 0) (7, 1) (7, 4) (5, 1) (1, 5) (6, 6) (1, 0) (1, 5) (7, 1) (1, 3) (4, 1)   (4, 3) (5, 4) (5, 1)

(2, 1) (4, 5) (6, 3) (1, 0) (7, 1) (7, 4)

(1, 2) (1, 0) (4, 3) (1, 5)   (4, 3) (3, 3) (7, 1) (6, 2)

© Carson-Dellosa CD-4309

65

Teach & Test Math: Grade 5

Polygons

Unit 5

A **polygon** is a three or more sided closed flat figure that exists on a plane.

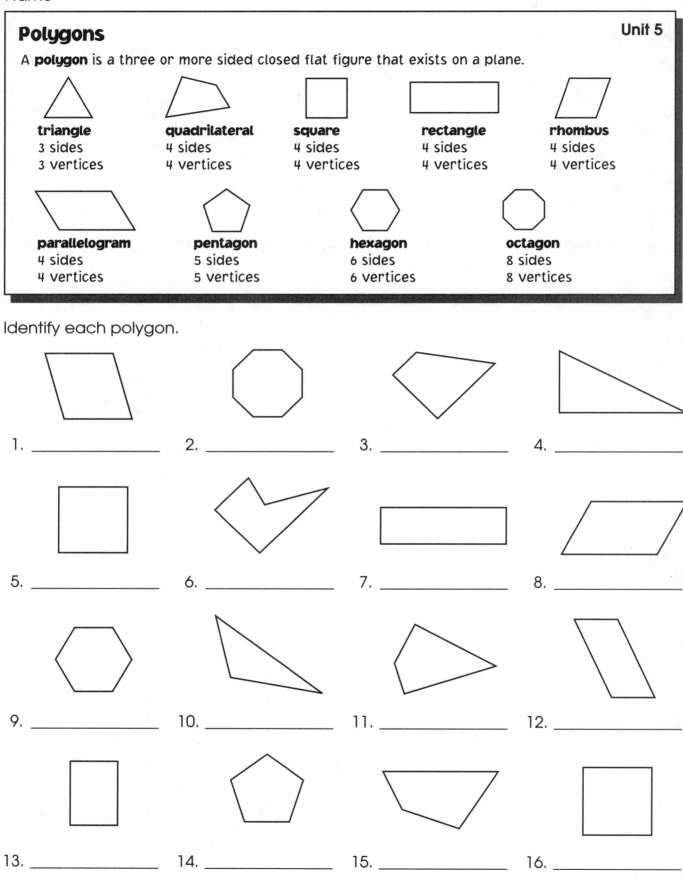

triangle
3 sides
3 vertices

quadrilateral
4 sides
4 vertices

square
4 sides
4 vertices

rectangle
4 sides
4 vertices

rhombus
4 sides
4 vertices

parallelogram
4 sides
4 vertices

pentagon
5 sides
5 vertices

hexagon
6 sides
6 vertices

octagon
8 sides
8 vertices

Identify each polygon.

1. _____

2. _____

3. _____

4. _____

5. _____

6. _____

7. _____

8. _____

9. _____

10. _____

11. _____

12. _____

13. _____

14. _____

15. _____

16. _____

Name

Perimeter

The **perimeter** is the distance around a polygon.

10 cm

3 cm   5 cm

10 cm

P = 10 cm + 3 cm + 10 cm + 5 cm
P = 28 cm

Find the perimeter of each polygon.

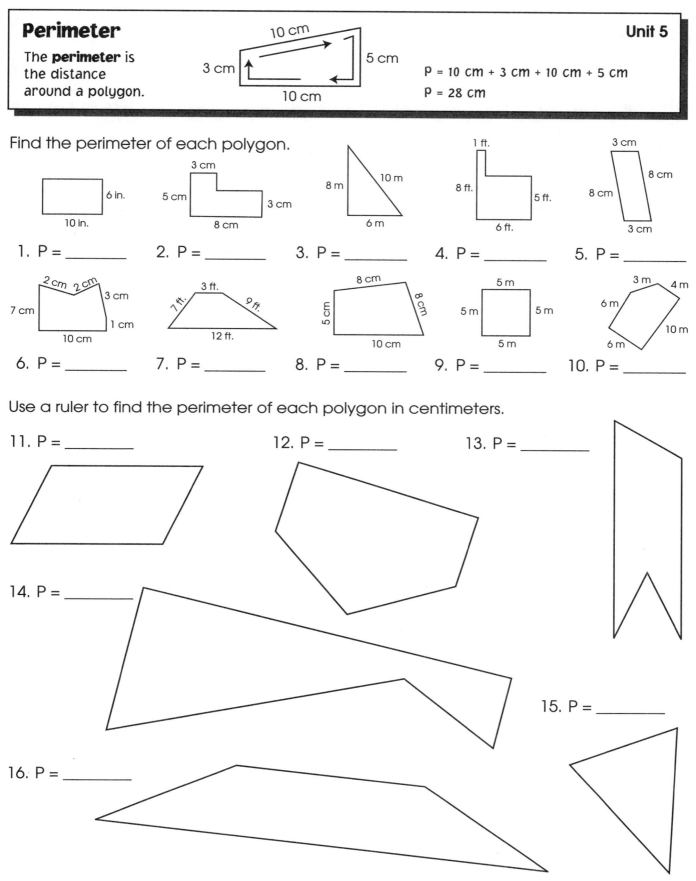

6 in.
10 in.

1. P = _____

3 cm
5 cm   3 cm
8 cm

2. P = _____

8 m   10 m
6 m

3. P = _____

1 ft.
8 ft.   5 ft.
6 ft.

4. P = _____

3 cm
8 cm
8 cm
3 cm

5. P = _____

2 cm 2 cm
7 cm   3 cm
1 cm
10 cm

6. P = _____

3 ft.
7 ft.   9 ft.
12 ft.

7. P = _____

8 cm
5 cm   8 cm
10 cm

8. P = _____

5 m
5 m   5 m
5 m

9. P = _____

3 m   4 m
6 m
10 m
6 m

10. P = _____

Use a ruler to find the perimeter of each polygon in centimeters.

11. P = _____

12. P = _____

13. P = _____

14. P = _____

15. P = _____

16. P = _____

Areas of rectangles and squares

Unit 5

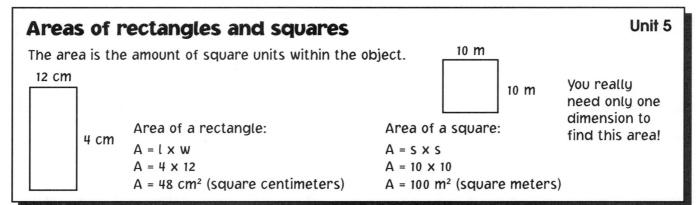

The area is the amount of square units within the object.

12 cm

4 cm

Area of a rectangle:

A = l x w

A = 4 x 12

A = 48 cm² (square centimeters)

10 m

10 m

Area of a square:

A = s x s

A = 10 x 10

A = 100 m² (square meters)

You really need only one dimension to find this area!

Find the area of each rectangle and square.

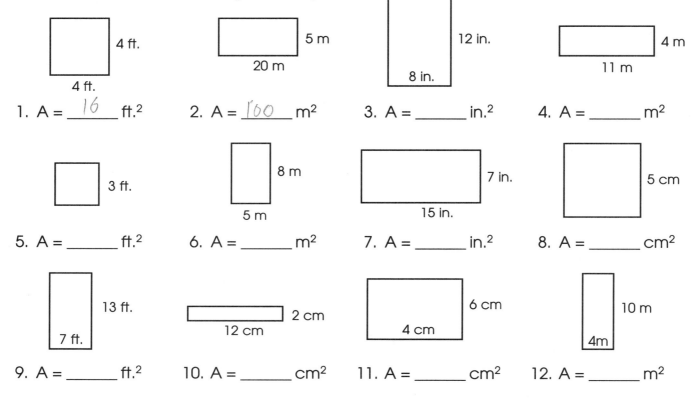

4 ft.

4 ft.

1. A = ___16___ ft.²

5 m

20 m

2. A = ___100___ m²

12 in.

8 in.

3. A = _____ in.²

4 m

11 m

4. A = _____ m²

3 ft.

5. A = _____ ft.²

8 m

5 m

6. A = _____ m²

7 in.

15 in.

7. A = _____ in.²

5 cm

8. A = _____ cm²

13 ft.

7 ft.

9. A = _____ ft.²

2 cm

12 cm

10. A = _____ cm²

6 cm

4 cm

11. A = _____ cm²

10 m

4m

12. A = _____ m²

Find the area of each rectangle and square. Use the lengths provided.

13. l = 10 m
    w = 7 m

    A = _____

14. l = 14 in.
    w = 6 in.

    A = _____

15. l = 8 m
    w = 5 m

    A = _____

16. l = 5 in.
    w = 5 in.

    A = _____

17. l = 7 m
    w = 7 m

    A = _____

18. l = 15 cm
    w = 2 cm

    A = _____

19. l = 11 m
    w = 6 m

    A = _____

20. l = 10 in.
    w = 7 in.

    A = _____

21. l = 18 cm
    w = 3 cm

    A = _____

22. l = 25 m
    w = 6 m

    A = _____

Name

Areas of right triangles   Unit 5

The area of a right triangle is actually one-half the area of a rectangle.

Two identical right triangles together create a rectangle.

Area of a right triangle:

$A = (b \times h) \div 2$
$A = (4 \times 5) \div 2$
$A = (20) \div 2$
$A = 10 \text{ cm}^2$

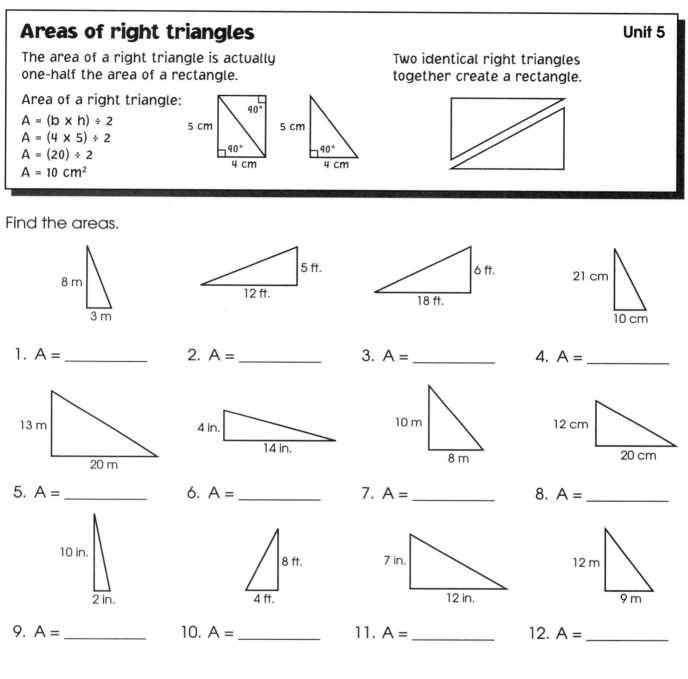

Find the areas.

1. A = _____

2. A = _____

3. A = _____

4. A = _____

5. A = _____

6. A = _____

7. A = _____

8. A = _____

9. A = _____

10. A = _____

11. A = _____

12. A = _____

Find the area of each right triangle. Use the lengths provided.

13. b = 3 in.
    h = 6 in.

    A = _____

14. b = 5 m
    h = 10 m

    A = _____

15. b = 7 ft.
    h = 10 ft.

    A = _____

16. b = 3 mm
    h = 8 mm

    A = _____

17. b = 6 m
    h = 8 m

    A = _____

18. b = 15 m
    h = 30 m

    A = _____

19. b = 3 cm
    h = 12 cm

    A = _____

20. b = 7 m
    h = 14 m

    A = _____

21. b = 3 mm
    h = 20 mm

    A = _____

22. b = 15 ft.
    h = 40 ft.

    A = _____

Name _____

Circles

A **chord** is a line segment that connects to two sides of a circle.

The **radius** is a line segment that extends from the center to any point on the outer edge of the circle.

2 cm

The **diameter** of a circle is a line segment that extends from one edge to the other passing through the center. It is twice the amount of the radius.

4 cm

The **circumference** of a circle is the distance around the outer edge. It is similar to the perimeter of a polygon.

The formula: 3.14 x diameter
                        3.14 x 6 cm

The circumference equals about 18.84 cm.

about 18.84 cm
6 cm

π stands for pi ≈ 3.14 (pronounced pie)

Identify each as a **chord**, **radius**, or **diameter**.

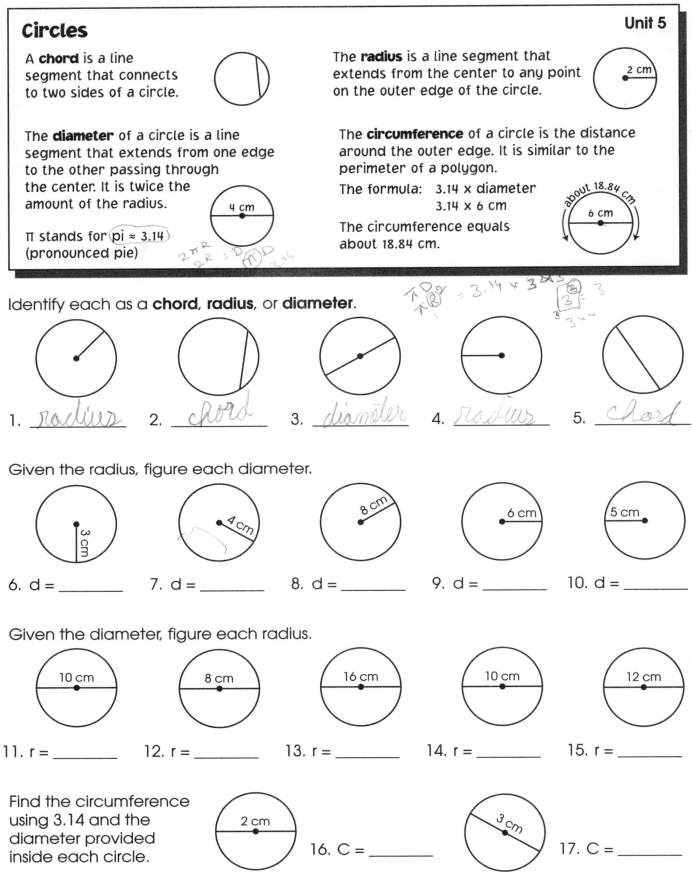

1. _radius_   2. _chord_   3. _diameter_   4. _radius_   5. _chord_

Given the radius, figure each diameter.

3 cm   4 cm   8 cm   6 cm   5 cm

6. d = _____   7. d = _____   8. d = _____   9. d = _____   10. d = _____

Given the diameter, figure each radius.

10 cm   8 cm   16 cm   10 cm   12 cm

11. r = _____   12. r = _____   13. r = _____   14. r = _____   15. r = _____

Find the circumference using 3.14 and the diameter provided inside each circle.

2 cm   16. C = _____

3 cm   17. C = _____

A = m² cm² ft²
V = m³ cm

Volume

Unit 5

The **volume** of a figure is the number of cubic units that are contained inside that object. In this example, cubic centimeters.

The formula:

$V = l \times w \times h$

$V = 6 \times 2 \times 5$

$V = 100$ cm³ Cu. Cm.
  60

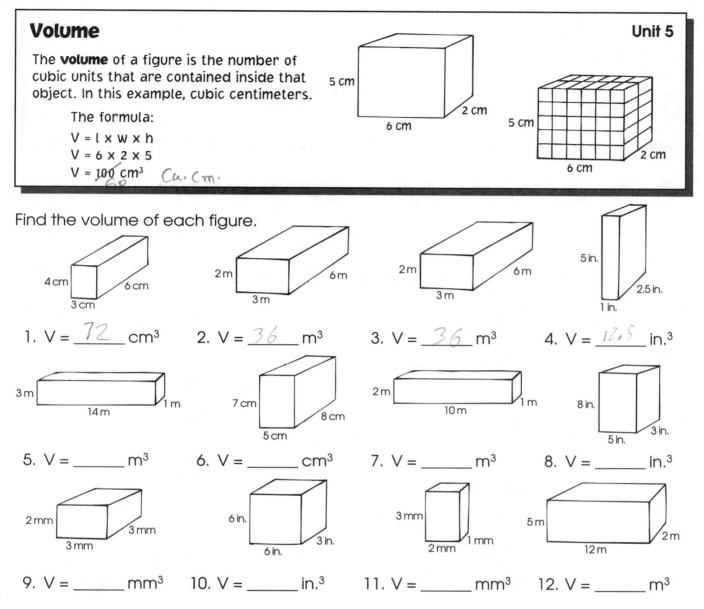

Find the volume of each figure.

1. $V = \underline{72}$ cm³

2. $V = \underline{36}$ m³

3. $V = \underline{36}$ m³

4. $V = \underline{12.5}$ in.³

5. $V = \underline{\hphantom{xxx}}$ m³

6. $V = \underline{\hphantom{xxx}}$ cm³

7. $V = \underline{\hphantom{xxx}}$ m³

8. $V = \underline{\hphantom{xxx}}$ in.³

9. $V = \underline{\hphantom{xxx}}$ mm³

10. $V = \underline{\hphantom{xxx}}$ in.³

11. $V = \underline{\hphantom{xxx}}$ mm³

12. $V = \underline{\hphantom{xxx}}$ m³

Given the dimensions, find the volume for each rectangular prism.

13. l = 2 cm
    w = 4 cm
    h = 3 cm

    V = _____

14. l = 5 m
    w = 3 m
    h = 4 m

    V = _____

15. l = 10 in.
    w = 3 in.
    h = 5 in.

    V = _____

16. l = 3.5 ft.
    w = 1 ft.
    h = 2 ft.

    V = _____

17. l = 4 m
    w = 2.5 m
    h = 6 m

    V = _____

18. l = 1 cm
    w = 20 cm
    h = 10 cm

    V = _____

19. l = 2 yd.
    w = 3 yd.
    h = 7 yd.

    V = _____

20. l = 10 cm
    w = 8 cm
    h = 2 cm

    V = _____

21. l = 3.4 m
    w = 2 m
    h = 5 m

    V = _____

22. l = 8 yd.
    w = 2 yd.
    h = 5 yd.

    V = _____

Similar and congruent

Figures that are the same shape but not the same size are **similar**.

Figures that are the same size and shape are **congruent**.

Draw a line to each set of similar figures.

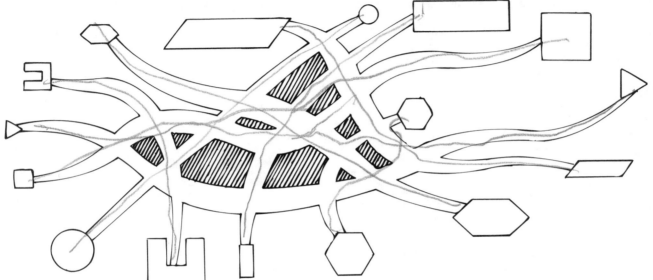

Draw a line to each set of congruent figures.

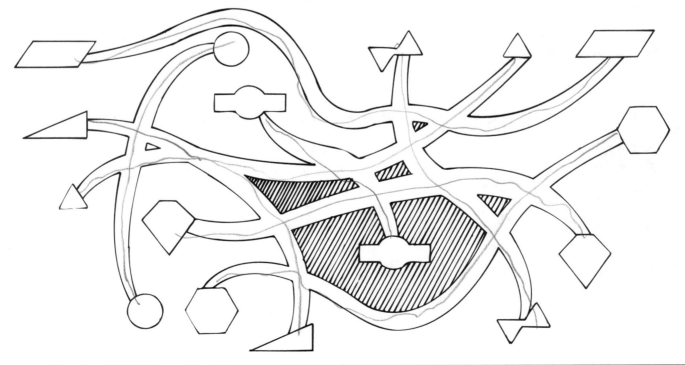

Unit 5 Test

Geometry

Read the question. Use an extra piece of paper to write problems down and solve them. Fill in the circle beside the best answer.

☐ Example:

How many congruent right triangles does it take to make a rectangle?

2   6   4   NG
(A)   (B)   (C)   (D)

5:48
5:53

Cross out answers you know are wrong.

Answer: It takes 2 because a rectangle divided diagonally creates two congruent triangles.

Now try these. You have 20 minutes. Continue until you see (STOP).

1. Complete this sentence: A plane is:

(A) a cube-shaped box

(B) a flat surface that goes out unending in all directions

(C) a parallelogram that floats

(D) NG

2. Identify.

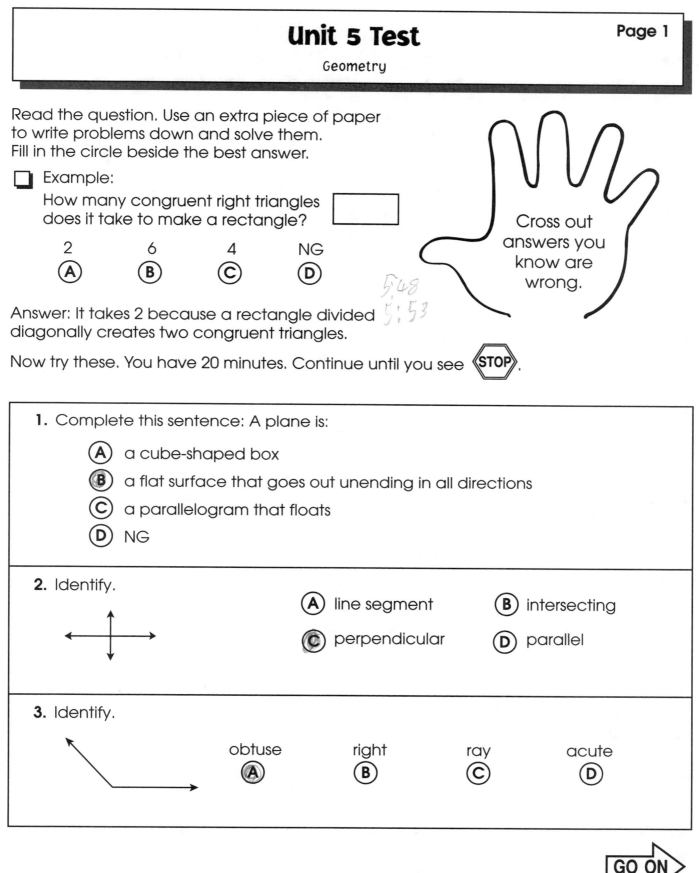

(A) line segment   (B) intersecting

(C) perpendicular   (D) parallel

3. Identify.

obtuse   right   ray   acute
(A)   (B)   (C)   (D)

GO ON

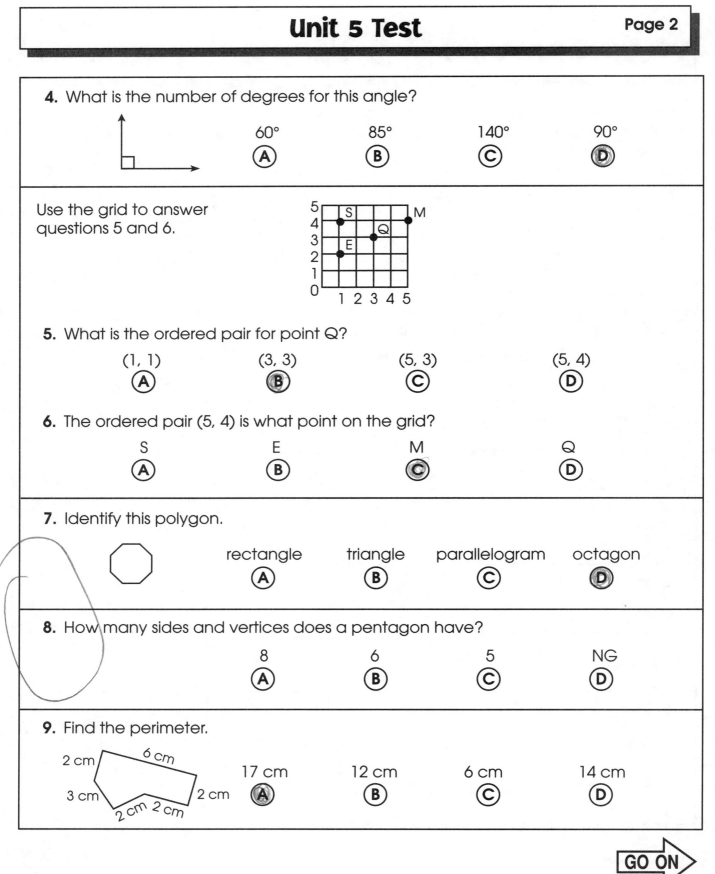

4. What is the number of degrees for this angle?

60°   85°   140°   90°
Ⓐ   Ⓑ   Ⓒ   Ⓓ

Use the grid to answer questions 5 and 6.

5. What is the ordered pair for point Q?

(1, 1)   (3, 3)   (5, 3)   (5, 4)
Ⓐ   Ⓑ   Ⓒ   Ⓓ

6. The ordered pair (5, 4) is what point on the grid?

S   E   M   Q
Ⓐ   Ⓑ   Ⓒ   Ⓓ

7. Identify this polygon.

rectangle   triangle   parallelogram   octagon
Ⓐ   Ⓑ   Ⓒ   Ⓓ

8. How many sides and vertices does a pentagon have?

8   6   5   NG
Ⓐ   Ⓑ   Ⓒ   Ⓓ

9. Find the perimeter.

2 cm   6 cm   3 cm   2 cm   2 cm   2 cm

17 cm   12 cm   6 cm   14 cm
Ⓐ   Ⓑ   Ⓒ   Ⓓ

GO ON

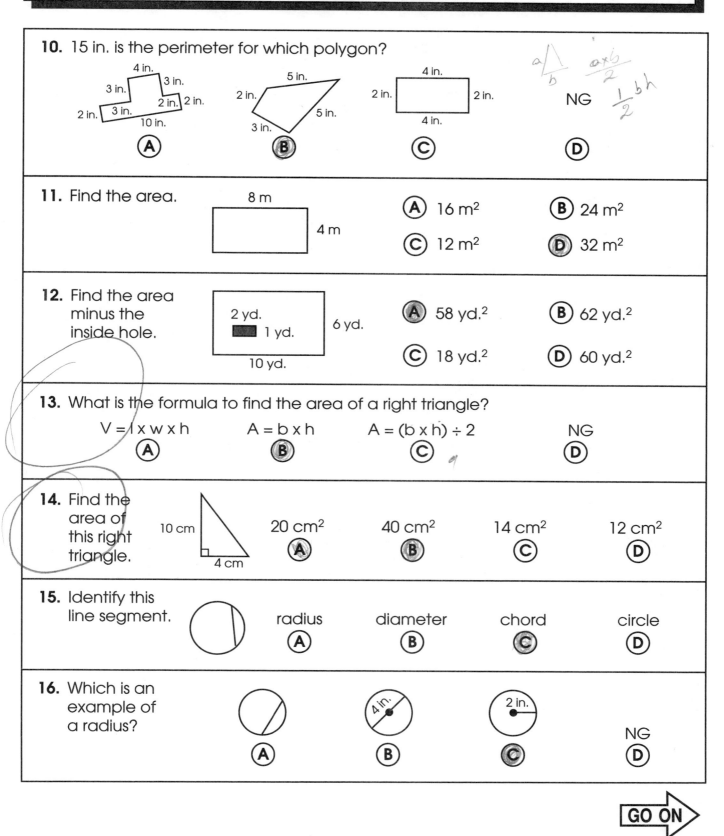

10. 15 in. is the perimeter for which polygon?

4 in.
3 in. 3 in.
3 in. 2 in. 2 in.
2 in. 3 in.
10 in.
(A)

5 in.
2 in.
5 in.
3 in.
(B)

4 in.
2 in. 2 in.
4 in.
(C)

NG
(D)

11. Find the area.

8 m
4 m

(A) 16 m²   (B) 24 m²

(C) 12 m²   (D) 32 m²

12. Find the area minus the inside hole.

2 yd.
1 yd.
6 yd.
10 yd.

(A) 58 yd.²   (B) 62 yd.²

(C) 18 yd.²   (D) 60 yd.²

13. What is the formula to find the area of a right triangle?

$V = l \times w \times h$ $A = b \times h$ $A = (b \times h) \div 2$ NG
(A)   (B)   (C)   (D)

14. Find the area of this right triangle.

10 cm
4 cm

20 cm²   40 cm²   14 cm²   12 cm²
(A)   (B)   (C)   (D)

15. Identify this line segment.

radius   diameter   chord   circle
(A)   (B)   (C)   (D)

16. Which is an example of a radius?

(A)   (B)   4 in.   (C) 2 in.   NG (D)

GO ON

Unit 5 Test

17. What is the volume of this figure?

2 cm

2 cm

4 cm

8 cm³
Ⓐ

16 cm³
Ⓑ

422 cm³
Ⓒ

6 cm³
Ⓓ

18. Figure the volume of a rectangular prism with these dimensions: l = 6 cm, w = 2 cm, and h = 3 cm.

36 cm³
Ⓐ

11 cm³
Ⓑ

15 cm³
Ⓒ

30 cm³
Ⓓ

19. Identify the similar figure.

Ⓐ

Ⓑ

Ⓒ

NG
Ⓓ

20. Identify the congruent figure.

Ⓐ

Ⓑ

Ⓒ

NG
Ⓓ

Why is a rectangle a type of quadrilateral?

It has four sides and four vertices.

Why can't a triangle ever be a quadrilateral?

I only has three angles and vertices.

STOP

Greatest common factors and lowest terms   Unit 6

$\frac{12}{16}$ In order to reduce fractions to lowest terms, it is best to find the greatest common factor that will divide evenly into both terms of the fraction.

Finding the greatest common factor for 12 and 16: First, find all the numbers that divide evenly into 12 and 16. These divisors are their factors.

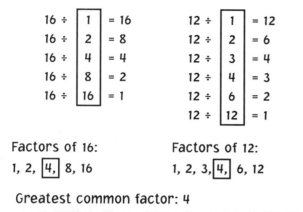

16 ÷	1	= 16
16 ÷	2	= 8
16 ÷	4	= 4
16 ÷	8	= 2
16 ÷	16	= 1

12 ÷	1	= 12
12 ÷	2	= 6
12 ÷	3	= 4
12 ÷	4	= 3
12 ÷	6	= 2
12 ÷	12	= 1

We can now reduce the fraction $^{12}/_{16}$ to lowest terms by dividing the numerator and denominator by 4, the greatest common factor.

$$\frac{12 \;\div\; 4}{16 \;\div\; 4} = \frac{3}{4}$$

Factors of 16:   Factors of 12:

1, 2, $\boxed{4,}$ 8, 16   1, 2, 3, $\boxed{4,}$ 6, 12

Greatest common factor: 4

Find the greatest common factors.

1. $\frac{10}{18}$ $\boxed{10}$ $\boxed{18}$

    GCF = __2__

2. $\frac{15}{20}$ $\boxed{15}$ $\boxed{20}$

    GCF = _____

3. $\frac{8}{40}$ $\boxed{8}$ $\boxed{40}$

    GCF = _____

4. $\frac{12}{24}$ $\boxed{12}$ $\boxed{24}$

    GCF = __4__

Reduce each fraction to lowest terms.

5. $\frac{14}{21}$ =

6. $\frac{10}{12}$ =

7. $\frac{16}{18}$ =

8. $\frac{12}{24}$ = $\frac{3}{6}$

9. $\frac{15}{25}$ =

10. $\frac{10}{24}$ =

11. $\frac{8}{12}$ =

12. $\frac{4}{10}$ =

13. $\frac{21}{28}$ =

14. $\frac{9}{18}$ =

15. $\frac{8}{24}$ =

16. $\frac{14}{20}$ =

17. $\frac{9}{27}$ =

18. $\frac{10}{18}$ = $\frac{5}{9}$

19. $\frac{16}{32}$ =

Name

Least common multiples and equivalent fractions   Unit 6

The purpose of a least common multiple in fractions is to find the least common denominator.

Let's look at the fractions: $1/3$ and $1/5$.
We need to look at the multiples of 3 and 5:

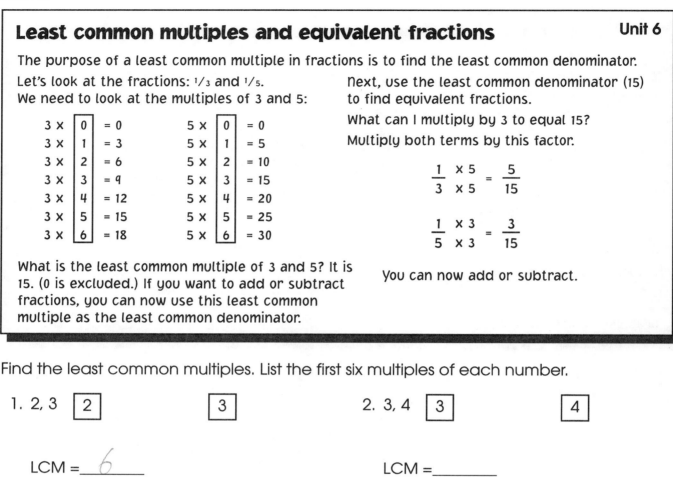

Next, use the least common denominator (15) to find equivalent fractions.

What can I multiply by 3 to equal 15?
Multiply both terms by this factor.

$$\frac{1}{3} \frac{\times 5}{\times 5} = \frac{5}{15}$$

$$\frac{1}{5} \frac{\times 3}{\times 3} = \frac{3}{15}$$

What is the least common multiple of 3 and 5? It is 15. (0 is excluded.) If you want to add or subtract fractions, you can now use this least common multiple as the least common denominator.

You can now add or subtract.

Find the least common multiples. List the first six multiples of each number.

1. 2, 3 [2]   [3]   2. 3, 4 [3]   [4]

   LCM = _6_   LCM = _____

3. 4, 5 [4]   [5]   4. 4, 6 [4]   [6]

   LCM = _20_   LCM = _____

Find the equivalent fractions and least common multiples.

5. $\frac{1}{2} = \frac{5}{10}$ $\frac{1}{5} = \frac{2}{10}$ 6. $\frac{1}{3} = $ $\frac{1}{4} = $ 7. $\frac{1}{2} = $ $\frac{1}{7} = $

   LCM = _10_   LCM = _____   LCM = _____

8. $\frac{1}{3} = $ $\frac{1}{8} = $ 9. $\frac{1}{5} = \frac{6}{30}$ $\frac{1}{6} = \frac{5}{30}$ 10. $\frac{1}{2} = $ $\frac{1}{9} = $

   LCM = _____   LCM = _30_   LCM = _____

11. $\frac{1}{3} = $ $\frac{1}{7} = $ 12. $\frac{1}{4} = $ $\frac{1}{7} = $ 13. $\frac{1}{3} = $ $\frac{1}{11} = $

    LCM = _____   LCM = _____   LCM = _____

Name

Addition of fractions   Unit 6

First, find the least
common denominator.

$$\frac{1}{3} + \frac{1}{4}$$

LCD = 12

Next, find the
equivalent fractions.

$$\frac{1}{3} \begin{array}{c} \times 4 \\ \times 4 \end{array} = \frac{4}{12}$$

$$\frac{1}{4} \begin{array}{c} \times 3 \\ \times 3 \end{array} = \frac{3}{12}$$

Last, add the numerators.

$$\frac{4}{12}$$
$$+ \frac{3}{12}$$
$$\overline{\frac{7}{12}}$$

Add. Reduce to lowest terms.

1. $\frac{1}{5}$
    $+ \frac{3}{5}$

2. $\frac{2}{8}$
    $+ \frac{3}{8}$

3. $\frac{3}{7}$
    $+ \frac{2}{7}$

4. $\frac{2}{5}$
    $+ \frac{3}{10}$
    $\frac{7}{10}$

5. $\frac{1}{2}$
    $+ \frac{1}{3}$

6. $\frac{1}{2}$
    $+ \frac{1}{5}$
    $\frac{7}{10}$

7. $\frac{1}{3}$
    $+ \frac{1}{7}$

8. $\frac{3}{4}$
    $+ \frac{1}{12}$

9. $\frac{1}{9}$
    $+ \frac{3}{18}$

10. $\frac{1}{2}$
    $+ \frac{5}{12}$

11. $\frac{1}{6}$
    $+ \frac{5}{18}$

12. $\frac{3}{9}$
    $+ \frac{2}{18}$

13. $\frac{2}{6}$
    $+ \frac{5}{12}$

14. $\frac{2}{7}$
    $+ \frac{3}{21}$

15. $\frac{1}{4}$
    $+ \frac{1}{5}$

Addition of mixed numbers

Find the least common denominator and equivalent fractions.	Add.	Reduce and regroup if necessary.

$3 \frac{2}{3}$ $\frac{2 \times 3}{3 \times 3} = \frac{6}{9}$

$+ 2 \frac{7}{9}$ $\frac{7 \times 1}{9 \times 1} = \frac{7}{9}$

$3 \frac{6}{9}$

$+ 2 \frac{7}{9}$
_____
$5 \frac{13}{9}$

$3 \frac{6}{9}$

$+ 2 \frac{7}{9}$
_____
$5 \frac{13}{9} = 6 \frac{4}{9}$

Add. Reduce to lowest terms.

1. $1 \frac{1}{5}$
    $+ 3 \frac{3}{5}$
    _____

2. $2 \frac{2}{5}$
    $+ 7 \frac{4}{10}$
    _____
    $9 \frac{8}{10}$

3. $5 \frac{2}{7}$
    $+ 4 \frac{5}{14}$
    _____
    $9 \frac{9}{14}$

4. $3 \frac{3}{10}$
    $+ 3 \frac{2}{10}$
    _____

5. $4 \frac{2}{3}$
    $+ 6 \frac{9}{12}$
    _____

6. $1 \frac{3}{4}$
    $+ 1 \frac{5}{8}$
    _____

7. $3 \frac{6}{9}$
    $+ 5 \frac{5}{9}$
    _____

8. $6 \frac{2}{4}$
    $+ \quad \frac{8}{12}$
    _____

9. $6 \frac{1}{2}$
    $+ 6 \frac{9}{10}$
    _____

10. $1 \frac{2}{3}$
    $+ 2 \frac{5}{6}$
    _____

11. $3 \frac{3}{5}$
    $+ 4 \frac{8}{15}$
    _____

12. $3 \frac{4}{6}$
    $+ 2 \frac{5}{12}$
    _____

Subtraction of fractions Unit 6

First, find the least common denominator.

$$\frac{3}{4} - \frac{2}{5}$$

LCD = 20

Next, find equivalent fractions.

$$\frac{3}{4} \times \frac{\times 5}{\times 5} = \frac{15}{20}$$

$$\frac{2}{5} \times \frac{\times 4}{\times 4} = \frac{8}{20}$$

Last, subtract.

$$\begin{array}{r} \frac{15}{20} \\ - \frac{8}{20} \\ \hline \frac{7}{20} \end{array}$$

Reduce to lowest terms if necessary.

Subtract. Reduce to lowest terms.

1. $\frac{4}{8} - \frac{2}{16} = \frac{6}{16}$

2. $\frac{4}{5} - \frac{1}{10} = \frac{7}{10}$

3. $\frac{6}{7} - \frac{5}{14}$

4. $\frac{2}{3} - \frac{1}{12}$

5. $\frac{5}{8} - \frac{2}{24}$

6. $\frac{1}{2} - \frac{3}{8}$

7. $\frac{2}{4} - \frac{3}{12}$

8. $\frac{1}{4} - \frac{1}{5}$

9. $\frac{12}{14} - \frac{8}{14}$

10. $\frac{3}{9} - \frac{6}{27}$

11. $\frac{6}{7} - \frac{5}{8}$

12. $\frac{8}{14} - \frac{2}{7}$

13. $\frac{3}{4} - \frac{4}{20}$

14. $\frac{7}{10} - \frac{1}{5}$

15. $\frac{18}{20} - \frac{2}{4}$

Subtraction of mixed numbers

Find the least common denominator and equivalent fractions.	Borrow and regroup. Subtract the fractions.	Subtract the whole numbers.	
$5\frac{1}{8}$ $\frac{1\times3}{8\times3}=\frac{3}{24}$	$5\frac{3}{24}$ $\overset{4}{\cancel{5}}\frac{\overset{27}{\cancel{3}}}{24}$	$\overset{4}{\cancel{5}}\frac{\overset{27}{\cancel{3}}}{24}$	Reduce to lowest terms if necessary.
$-2\frac{1}{3}$ $\frac{1\times8}{3\times8}=\frac{8}{24}$	$-2\frac{8}{24}$ $-2\frac{8}{24}$	$-2\frac{8}{24}$	
	$\frac{19}{24}$	$2\frac{19}{24}$	

Subtract. Reduce to lowest terms.

1. $6\frac{1}{4}$
   $-3\frac{5}{8}$

2. $9\frac{1}{5}$
   $-4\frac{6}{10}$
   $4\frac{6}{10}$

3. $2\frac{1}{10}$
   $-1\frac{4}{5}$

4. $9\frac{4}{7}$
   $-\frac{8}{14}$

5. $8\frac{5}{9}$
   $-2\frac{2}{3}$

6. $5\frac{1}{2}$
   $-\frac{3}{4}$

7. $6\frac{4}{9}$
   $-2\frac{3}{18}$

8. $10\frac{2}{3}$
   $-5\frac{18}{27}$

9. $7\frac{2}{5}$
   $-3\frac{1}{2}$

10. $10\frac{1}{2}$
   $-8\frac{6}{7}$

11. $7\frac{1}{3}$
   $-3\frac{4}{12}$

12. $6\frac{1}{3}$
   $-4\frac{3}{4}$

13. $5\frac{1}{7}$
   $-3\frac{1}{5}$

14. $8\frac{2}{3}$
   $-5\frac{1}{7}$

15. $9\frac{1}{2}$
   $-\frac{5}{8}$

16. $18\frac{1}{3}$
   $-\frac{3}{4}$

Name

Subtraction of fractions from whole numbers   Unit 6

Borrow and regroup.

$$3 \qquad 2\cancel{3}\dfrac{9}{9}$$
$$-\dfrac{6}{9} \qquad -\dfrac{6}{9}$$

Subtract.

$$2\cancel{3}\dfrac{9}{9}$$
$$-\dfrac{6}{9}$$
$$\overline{\quad 2\dfrac{3}{9}}$$

Reduce to lowest terms.

$$2\dfrac{3}{9} = 2\dfrac{1}{3}$$

Subtract. Reduce to lowest terms.

1. $6\ \overset{5}{\cancel{}}\ \dfrac{\overset{8}{\cancel{8}}}{\cancel{8}}$
   $-\dfrac{3}{8}$
   $5\dfrac{5}{8}$

2. $5\ \overset{4}{\cancel{}}\ \dfrac{\overset{14}{\cancel{14}}}{\cancel{14}}$
   $-\dfrac{2}{14}$
   $4\dfrac{12}{14}$

3. 12
   $-\dfrac{5}{16}$

4. 8
   $-\dfrac{3}{7}$

5. 27
   $-\dfrac{14}{20}$

6. 10
   $-\dfrac{7}{15}$

7. 8
   $-\dfrac{3}{5}$

8. 14
   $-\dfrac{5}{6}$

9. 52
   $-\dfrac{3}{27}$

10. 15
    $-\dfrac{5}{6}$

11. 42
    $-\dfrac{7}{8}$

12. 21
    $-\dfrac{3}{4}$

13. 50
    $-\dfrac{3}{8}$

14. 61
    $-\dfrac{5}{9}$

15. 3
    $-\dfrac{2}{16}$

16. 9
    $-\dfrac{3}{7}$

Multiplication of whole numbers and fractions

Unit 6

When multiplying whole numbers and fractions:

$7 \times \frac{3}{7}$

Convert the whole number to a fraction. Multiply straight across.

$\frac{7}{1} \times \frac{3}{7} = \frac{21}{7}$

Convert answer to a whole number.

$\frac{21}{7} = 3$

Example: $7 \times \frac{2}{3}$

Multiply straight across.

$\frac{7}{1} \times \frac{2}{3} = \frac{14}{3}$

If the product is an improper fraction, convert to a mixed number in lowest terms.

$\frac{14}{3} = 4\frac{2}{3}$

Multiply. Reduce to lowest terms.

1. $3 \times \frac{2}{4} = 1\frac{2}{4}$

2. $\frac{1}{2} \times \frac{3}{8} = \frac{3}{16}$

3. $\frac{1}{5} \times \frac{3}{8}$

4. $5 \times \frac{2}{7}$

5. $\frac{3}{7} \times \frac{2}{4}$

6. $\frac{5}{9} \times \frac{2}{3}$

7. $\frac{1}{2} \times \frac{5}{8}$

8. $12 \times \frac{1}{3}$

9. $\frac{2}{7} \times 4$

10. $15 \times \frac{1}{5}$

11. $\frac{1}{3} \times \frac{2}{5}$

12. $\frac{1}{8} \times 4$

13. $\frac{5}{7} \times \frac{1}{3}$

14. $\frac{2}{6} \times \frac{1}{2}$

15. $\frac{3}{5} \times \frac{1}{4}$

16. $\frac{2}{7} \times \frac{1}{4}$

17. $\frac{3}{9} \times \frac{2}{5}$

18. $\frac{1}{3} \times \frac{2}{8}$

19. $5 \times \frac{1}{4}$

20. $6 \times \frac{3}{6}$

Multiplication of mixed numbers   Unit 6

Convert the mixed numbers to fractions.

$$1\frac{1}{3} \times 2\frac{1}{2} = \frac{4}{3} \times \frac{5}{2}$$

Multiply.

$$\frac{4}{3} \times \frac{5}{2} = \frac{20}{6}$$

Convert the product back to a mixed number in lowest terms.

$$\frac{20}{6} = 3\frac{2}{6} = 3\frac{1}{3}$$

Multiply. Reduce to lowest terms.

1. $1\frac{1}{2} \times 3 = 4\frac{1}{2}$

2. $1\frac{3}{4} \times \frac{1}{3}$

3. $\frac{3}{5} \times 1\frac{2}{3}$

4. $1\frac{3}{8} \times 2\frac{1}{5}$

5. $2\frac{1}{3} \times 5$

6. $3\frac{1}{2} \times 1\frac{1}{8}$

7. $9 \times 1\frac{2}{4}$

8. $1\frac{4}{6} \times \frac{3}{4}$

9. $3\frac{1}{4} \times 2\frac{1}{3}$

10. $4\frac{3}{8} \times 2\frac{1}{5}$

11. $1\frac{1}{3} \times 2\frac{1}{2}$

12. $1\frac{1}{5} \times 2\frac{3}{4}$

13. $\frac{7}{9} \times 1\frac{1}{3}$

14. $1\frac{1}{2} \times 8$

15. $2\frac{1}{6} \times 4$

Write a story problem that uses a mixed number in the problem.

Mixed Numbers

Division of whole numbers by fractions

$4 \div \frac{1}{4}$

Divide each figure into fourths.

$4 \div \frac{1}{4} = 16$ There are now 16 parts.

To solve, turn the division problem into a multiplication problem by flipping the digits in the fraction.

$4 \times \frac{4}{1} = 16$

Check your quotient by multiplying it by the divisor.

$16 \times \frac{1}{4} = 4$

$\frac{16}{4} = 4$

Divide.

1. $5 \div \frac{1}{3} = 5 \times \frac{3}{1} =$

2. $4 \div \frac{1}{6} = \frac{24}{6}$

3. $2 \div \frac{1}{2} = \frac{4}{2}$

4. $7 \div \frac{1}{5}$

5. $3 \div \frac{1}{4}$

6. $5 \div \frac{1}{5}$

7. $4 \div \frac{1}{3}$

8. $3 \div \frac{1}{2}$

9. $4 \div \frac{1}{4}$

10. $2 \div \frac{1}{4}$

11. $4 \div \frac{1}{2}$

12. $3 \div \frac{1}{3}$

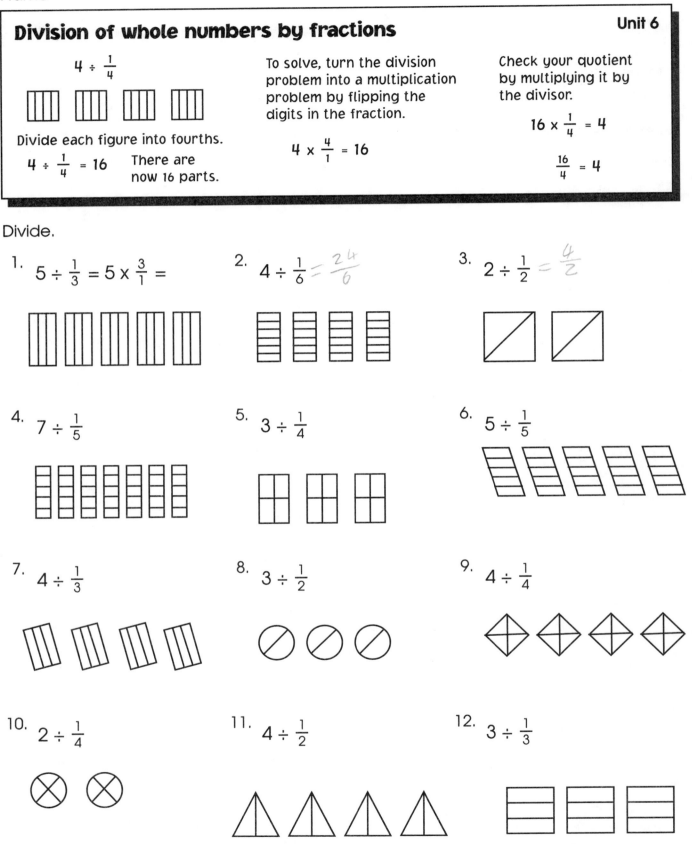

Name

Unit 6 Test

Fractions

Read the question. Use an extra piece of paper to write problems down and solve them. Fill in the circle beside the best answer.

☐ Example:

Reduce the fraction to lowest terms. $\frac{15}{30}$

$\frac{1}{2}$ $\frac{5}{6}$ $\frac{3}{7}$ NG

Ⓐ   Ⓑ   Ⓒ   Ⓓ

Answer: A because $^{15}/_{30}$ when divided by its greatest common factor (15) equals ½.

Now try these. You have 20 minutes.

Continue until you see ⬡STOP.

Always read the question twice. Does your answer make sense?

1. Reduce $\frac{10}{40}$ to lowest terms.	$\frac{4}{10}$ Ⓐ	$\frac{5}{20}$ Ⓑ	$\frac{2}{8}$ Ⓒ	$\frac{1}{4}$ Ⓓ
2. The greatest common factor of $\frac{10}{20}$ is:	5 Ⓐ	10 Ⓑ	8 Ⓒ	NG Ⓓ
3. The least common multiple for 2 and 3 is:	6 Ⓐ	7 Ⓑ	13 Ⓒ	NG Ⓓ
4. $\frac{2}{4}$ is an equivalent fraction for:	$\frac{5}{6}$ Ⓐ	$\frac{1}{2}$ Ⓑ	$\frac{8}{15}$ Ⓒ	$\frac{4}{5}$ Ⓓ

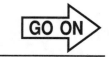

5.

$\frac{2}{8}$
$+ \frac{3}{8}$

$\frac{5}{16}$ (A) $\frac{3}{8}$ (B) $\frac{2}{8}$ (C) $\frac{5}{8}$ (D)

6.

$\frac{1}{2}$
$+ \frac{1}{5}$

$\frac{2}{5}$ (A) $\frac{1}{3}$ (B) $\frac{7}{10}$ (C) $\frac{3}{10}$ (D)

7. What is the first step to adding this problem of mixed numbers?

$1\frac{2}{4}$

$+ 2\frac{1}{8}$

(A) Find the least common denominator and make equivalent fractions.

(B) Add the whole numbers.

(C) Regroup.

(D) NG

8.

$1\frac{3}{5}$
$+ 2\frac{1}{15}$

$3\frac{4}{15}$ (A) $3\frac{2}{3}$ (B) $4\frac{4}{5}$ (C) NG (D)

9.

$\frac{5}{6}$
$- \frac{1}{12}$

$\frac{4}{12}$ (A) $\frac{4}{6}$ (B) $\frac{3}{4}$ (C) $\frac{11}{12}$ (D)

10.

$\frac{1}{2}$
$- \frac{1}{8}$

$\frac{3}{8}$ (A) $\frac{1}{6}$ (B) $\frac{4}{8}$ (C) $\frac{5}{8}$ (D)

GO ON

11. What is the last step to subtracting this problem of mixed numbers?

$$6\frac{1}{4}$$
$$-\ 2\frac{1}{8}$$

(A) Subtract the whole numbers.

(B) Find the least common denominator.

(C) Regroup.

(D) NG

12.

$$7\frac{5}{8}$$
$$-\ \frac{11}{16}$$

$7\frac{6}{16}$ $6\frac{15}{16}$ 4 $7\frac{15}{16}$

(A)   (B)   (C)   (D)

13. When subtracting, what fraction will I carry over to regroup?

$$\cancel{16}\,\square^{15}$$
$$-\ \frac{3}{8}$$

$\frac{8}{16}$ $\frac{15}{8}$ $\frac{3}{8}$ NG

(A)   (B)   (C)   (D)

14.

$$5$$
$$-\ \frac{3}{4}$$

$4\frac{1}{4}$ $5\frac{1}{4}$ $5\frac{3}{4}$ $4\frac{3}{4}$

(A)   (B)   (C)   (D)

15. Convert the whole number 8 to a fraction.

$\frac{8}{8}$ $\frac{8}{1}$ $\frac{1}{8}$ NG

(A)   (B)   (C)   (D)

16.

$$5\ \times\ \frac{2}{5}$$

$\frac{10}{25}$ 2 $\frac{2}{25}$ $\frac{2}{5}$

(A)   (B)   (C)   (D)

GO ON

Unit 6 Test

17. $5 \times 1\frac{1}{2}$

    $7\frac{1}{2}$ $7\frac{2}{5}$ $\frac{3}{10}$ $6\frac{1}{2}$

    (A)   (B)   (C)   (D)

18. $1\frac{1}{2} \times 2\frac{1}{2}$

    $3\frac{3}{4}$ $2\frac{1}{2}$ $1\frac{1}{2}$ 4

    (A)   (B)   (C)   (D)

19. Which diagram correctly displays $3 \div \frac{1}{2}$?

(A)   (B)   (C)   (D) NG

20. $3 \div \frac{1}{4}$

    12 6 7 4

    (A)   (B)   (C)   (D)

Explain in your own words why $4 \div \frac{1}{3} = 12$

A. What does the 4 stand for?

B. What does the divisor $\frac{1}{3}$ do?

C. What does the 12 stand for?

_____

_____

_____

_____

_____

STOP

Addition and subtraction of time

60 seconds (s) = 1 minute (min)
60 minutes = 1 hour (h)
24 hours = 1 day (d)
7 days = 1 week (wk)
365 ¼ days = 1 year (yr)
52 weeks = 1 year

Addition of time:

```
   12 min   45 s
+   8 min   21 s
            66 s
```

Add the seconds. 66 seconds equal 1 minute and 6 seconds. Since you have more than 60 seconds, which equals 1 minute, regroup. Add the minutes.

```
   12 min   45 s
+   8 min   21 s
   21 min    6 s
```

Subtraction of time:

```
   12 h   21 min
 −  7 h   40 min
```

You cannot take 40 minutes from 21 minutes. Borrow and regroup. One hour equals 60 minutes. Add these to the minutes. Subtract the minutes.

```
   ¹¹1̶2̶ h   ⁸¹2̶1̶ min   (21 + 60 = 81)
 −   7 h     40 min
            41 min
```

Subtract the hours.

```
   ¹¹1̶2̶ h   ⁸¹2̶1̶ min
 −   7 h     40 min
     4 h     41 min
```

Add.

1.
```
    3 h   42 min
+   8 h   25 min
```

2.
```
   14 min   45 s
+  21 min   20 s
```

3.
```
   15 min   20 s
+  15 min   41 s
```

4.
```
    2 h   21 min
+   7 h   52 min
```

5.
```
   25 min   10 s
+  15 min   58 s
```

6.
```
   10 h   35 min
+   2 h   35 min
```

Subtract.

7.
```
   27 h   15 min
 −  8 h   25 min
```

8.
```
    2 min   10 s
 −  1 min   59 s
```

9.
```
    8 h   40 s
 −  6 h   50 s
```

10.
```
    3 h   32 min
 −  1 h   48 min
```

11.
```
    4 min   15 s
 −  2 min   25 s
```

12.
```
    8 min   45 s
 −  1 min   55 s
```

Metric units of length

1 centimeter (cm) = 10 millimeters (mm)
1 meter (m) = 100 centimeters
1 kilometer (km) = 1,000 meters

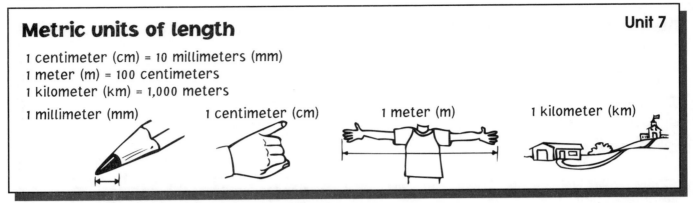

Draw the following lengths using a metric ruler.

1. 3 cm

2. 3.5 cm

3. 2.5 cm

4. 5 cm

5. 0.5 cm

6. 1 cm

7. 4.5 cm

8. 2 cm

9. 6.5 cm

10. 6 cm

11. 1.5 cm

12. 4 cm

Compare using >, <, and =.

13. 4 mm $\bigcirc$ 4 cm

14. 1 km $\bigcirc$ 1,000 m

15. 2 m $\bigcirc$ 200 cm

16. 4 m $\bigcirc$ 50 cm

17. 1 m $\bigcirc$ 150 cm

18. 3 km $\bigcirc$ 3 m

19. 100 mm $\bigcirc$ 10 cm

20. 10 km $\bigcirc$ 20 m

21. 3 cm $\bigcirc$ 35 mm

22. 5 cm $\bigcirc$ 10 mm

23. 1 km $\bigcirc$ 300 m

24. 2 km $\bigcirc$ 2,000 m

25. 5 cm $\bigcirc$ 55 mm

26. 2 m $\bigcirc$ 100 cm

27. 8 km $\bigcirc$ 8 m

Name

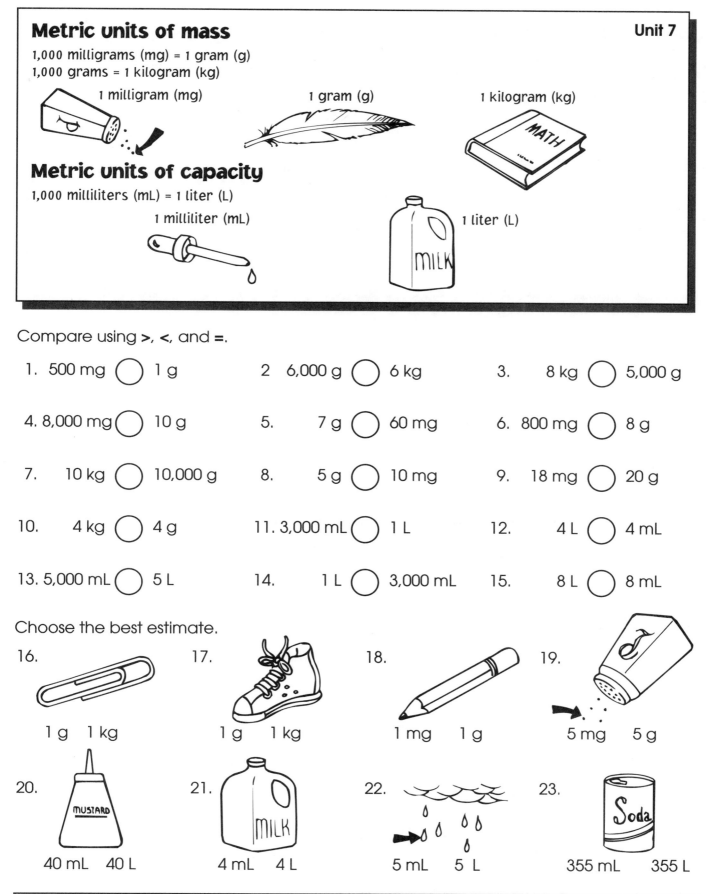

Metric units of mass   Unit 7

1,000 milligrams (mg) = 1 gram (g)
1,000 grams = 1 kilogram (kg)

1 milligram (mg)   1 gram (g)   1 kilogram (kg)

Metric units of capacity

1,000 milliliters (mL) = 1 liter (L)

1 milliliter (mL)   1 liter (L)

Compare using >, <, and =.

1. 500 mg ◯ 1 g   2 6,000 g ◯ 6 kg   3.   8 kg ◯ 5,000 g

4. 8,000 mg ◯ 10 g   5.   7 g ◯ 60 mg   6. 800 mg ◯ 8 g

7. 10 kg ◯ 10,000 g   8.   5 g ◯ 10 mg   9. 18 mg ◯ 20 g

10.   4 kg ◯ 4 g   11. 3,000 mL ◯ 1 L   12.   4 L ◯ 4 mL

13. 5,000 mL ◯ 5 L   14.   1 L ◯ 3,000 mL   15.   8 L ◯ 8 mL

Choose the best estimate.

16.   17.   18.   19.

1 g   1 kg   1 g   1 kg   1 mg   1 g   5 mg   5 g

20.   21.   22.   23.

40 mL   40 L   4 mL   4 L   5 mL   5 L   355 mL   355 L

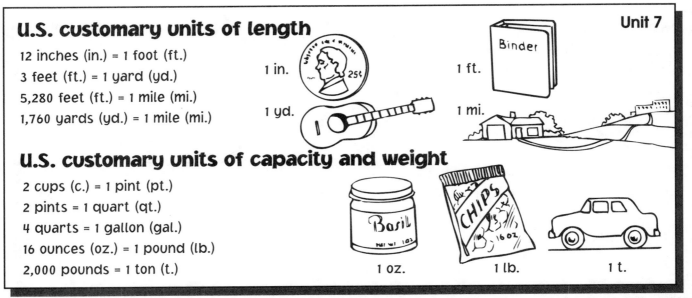

U.S. customary units of length

Unit 7

12 inches (in.) = 1 foot (ft.)

3 feet (ft.) = 1 yard (yd.)

5,280 feet (ft.) = 1 mile (mi.)

1,760 yards (yd.) = 1 mile (mi.)

1 in.

1 yd.

1 ft.

1 mi.

U.S. customary units of capacity and weight

2 cups (c.) = 1 pint (pt.)

2 pints = 1 quart (qt.)

4 quarts = 1 gallon (gal.)

16 ounces (oz.) = 1 pound (lb.)

2,000 pounds = 1 ton (t.)

1 oz.

1 lb.

1 t.

Using an inch ruler, figure the lengths in inches.

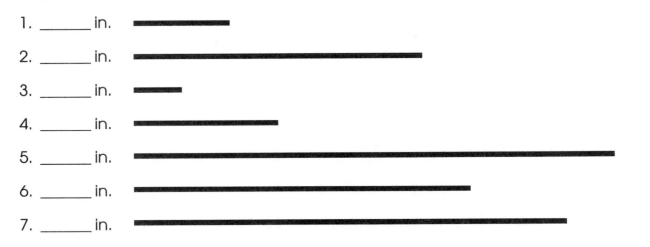

1. _____ in.

2. _____ in.

3. _____ in.

4. _____ in.

5. _____ in.

6. _____ in.

7. _____ in.

Convert.

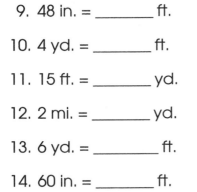
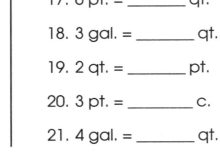
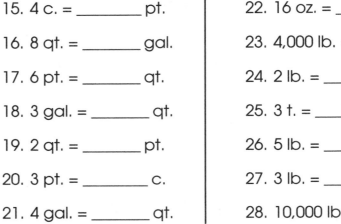
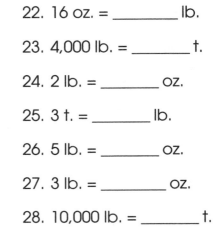

Length	Capacity	Weight
8. 3 ft. = _____ in.	15. 4 c. = _____ pt.	22. 16 oz. = _____ lb.
9. 48 in. = _____ ft.	16. 8 qt. = _____ gal.	23. 4,000 lb. = _____ t.
10. 4 yd. = _____ ft.	17. 6 pt. = _____ qt.	24. 2 lb. = _____ oz.
11. 15 ft. = _____ yd.	18. 3 gal. = _____ qt.	25. 3 t. = _____ lb.
12. 2 mi. = _____ yd.	19. 2 qt. = _____ pt.	26. 5 lb. = _____ oz.
13. 6 yd. = _____ ft.	20. 3 pt. = _____ c.	27. 3 lb. = _____ oz.
14. 60 in. = _____ ft.	21. 4 gal. = _____ qt.	28. 10,000 lb. = _____ t.

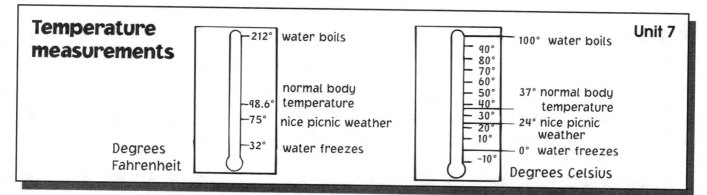

Figure the temperature movement in degrees Fahrenheit.

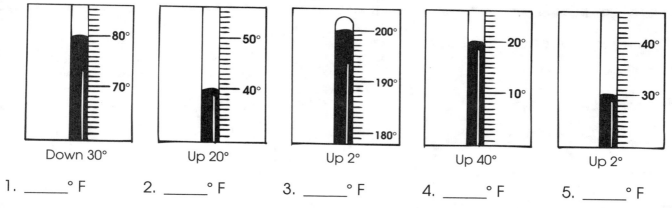

| Down 30° | Up 20° | Up 2° | Up 40° | Up 2° |

1. _____° F   2. _____° F   3. _____° F   4. _____° F   5. _____° F

Figure the temperature movement in degrees Celsius.

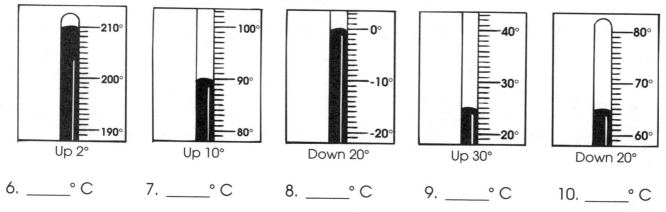

| Up 2° | Up 10° | Down 20° | Up 30° | Down 20° |

6. _____° C   7. _____° C   8. _____° C   9. _____° C   10. _____° C

Answer the questions.

11. How far away in degrees Fahrenheit is our normal body temperature (98.6° F) from water freezing (32° F)? _____

12. In degrees Fahrenheit, what is the difference in temperature between water freezing (32° F) and water boiling (212° F)? _____

13. In degrees Celsius, what is the difference in degrees from water freezing (0° C) to water boiling (100° C)? _____

Range, median, and mode

Data: 3, 5, 8, 10, 12, 12, 12

When you have a group of data, the difference between the least and the greatest is the **range**. Range: $12 - 3 = 9$

When data is arranged in order, the number in the middle of your data is the **median**.

3, 5, 8, $\boxed{10,}$ 12, 12, 12   The median is 10.

The most frequent or common number that occurs in your data is called the **mode**. The most frequent occurring number in this data is 12.

note: if the median number is the two inside numbers, add them together and divide by 2.

Example: 2, 3, 4, 4, 5, 6

$$4 + 4 = 8$$

$$\begin{array}{r} 4 \\ 2\,\overline{\smash{)}\,8} \\ -\,8 \\ \hline 0 \end{array}$$ Median = 4

Find the range in each set of data.

1. 3.6, 4.9, 6.7, 7.9 _____

2. 7 L, 9 L, 10 L, 12 L, 15 L _____

3. 2 mm, 4 mm, 6 mm _____

4. 2 ft., 5 ft., 7 ft., 12 ft. _____

5. 22.5, 45.6, 67.8, 98.6 _____

6. 121 lb., 134 lb., 456 lb. _____

7. 3 m, 5 m, 8 m, 13 m, 16 m _____

8. 12, 16, 18, 20, 21 _____

Find the median in each set of data.

9. 2, 3, 4, 5, 6, 7, 8 _____

10. 56 m, 67 m, 87 m, 99 m, 123 m _____

11. 10 mL, 12 mL, 14 mL, 16 mL, 18 mL _____

12. 2, 3, 4, 5, 6, 7 _____

13. 12 oz., 14 oz., 18 oz., 22 oz. _____

14. 2 t., 4 t., 6 t., 8 t., 10 t. _____

Find the mode in each set of data.

15. 3 in., 4 in., 4 in., 5 in., 6 in. _____

16. 23, 24, 25, 25, 26, 26, 26, 27, 28 _____

17. 34, 34, 34, 36, 36, 36, 36 _____

18. 1, 1, 1, 1, 1, 1, 2, 2, 2, 3, 3, 3, 3 _____

Find the range and median for each set of data.

19. Range: _____

    Median: _____

20. Range: _____

    Median: _____

21. Range: _____

    Median: _____

Name _____

Mean   Unit 7

To arrive at the **mean** (average), simply add
together the data in the group and divide the
sum by the number of data entries.

Example: 2, 2, 2, 3, 4, 5

$2 + 2 + 2 + 3 + 4 + 5 = 18$

$$6\overline{)18}$$ with quotient 3, -18, 0 Mean = 3

Find the mean.

1. David's free throw points for each game: 10, 14, 22, 15, 18 mean: _____

2. Sam's weekly chess game wins: 8, 4, 6, 9, 12, 6 mean: _____

3. Monica's weekly gifts to the food bank: 21, 35, 44, 12, 81 mean: _____

4. Eva's weekly math test scores: 89%, 95%, 100%, 98%, 97% mean: _____

5. Mark's completed drawings each week: 4, 6, 5, 3, 1, 8 mean: _____

6. Steve's weekly car sales: 3, 8, 10, 4, 0, 5 mean: _____

7. Watermelon seeds: 25, 42, 51, 35 mean: _____

8. Orange seeds: 8, 7, 2, 4, 3, 5, 6 mean: _____

9. Team home runs: 8, 4, 6, 10, 14, 15 mean: _____

10. Bill's bowling scores: 125, 100, 200, 140, 180 mean: _____

11. Daily hits at Gwen's cooking internet site: 52, 81, 46, 149, 22 mean: _____

12. Dog ownership at Mathiscool Elementary School:
    K = 65, 1st = 82, 2nd = 59, 3rd = 66, 4th = 82, 5th = 159, 6th = 68 mean: _____

Find the mean.

13. 3, 6, 17, 21, 35 _____

14. 45, 48, 49, 51, 53 _____

15. 213, 245, 256, 266 _____

16. 10, 13, 15, 18, 21, 24, 25 _____

17. 81, 84, 86, 91 _____

18. 2, 2, 2, 2, 3, 4 _____

19. 321, 412, 523, 611, 713 _____

20. 32, 33, 34, 35, 36 _____

21. 3, 4, 5, 6, 7, 8, 9 _____

22. 2.3, 4.5, 5.2, 7.1 _____

23. 10.2, 10.3, 10.5, 10.8 _____

24. 5.7, 5.7, 6.8, 9.4 _____

25. 1.2, 3.4, 6.7, 10.2, 12.4 _____

26. 1.23, 3.64, 5.12 _____

Name

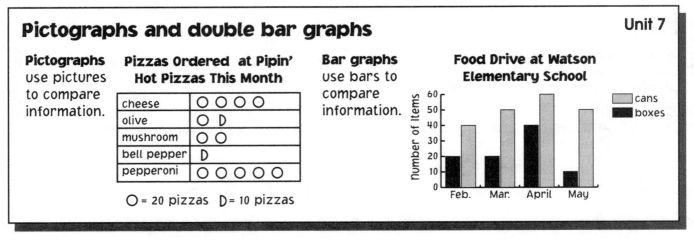

Pictographs and double bar graphs

Pictographs use pictures to compare information.

Pizzas Ordered at Pipin' Hot Pizzas This Month

cheese	O O O O
olive	O D
mushroom	O O
bell pepper	D
pepperoni	O O O O O

O = 20 pizzas   D = 10 pizzas

Bar graphs use bars to compare information.

Food Drive at Watson Elementary School

cans / boxes

Use the graphs to answer each question.

Favorite Frozen Fruitsicles at Armstrong Elementary

Grape Juice	‑D ‑D ‑ᴆ
Orange Juice	‑D ‑D ‑ᴆ
Cranberry Juice	‑D ‑D ‑D
Cherry Juice	‑D ‑D ‑D ‑D
Strawberry Juice	‑D ‑D ‑D ‑D ‑D
Kiwi Juice	‑D ‑D ‑D
Apple Juice	‑D

‑D = 4 frozen fruitsicles

‑ᴆ = 2 frozen fruitsicles

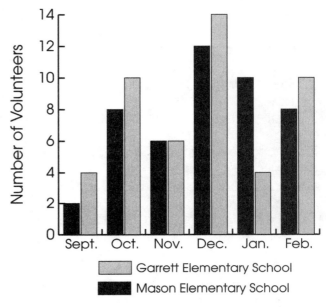

Food Bank Volunteers

Garrett Elementary School
Mason Elementary School

1. Which flavor is the most popular?

   _____

2. Which two flavors are half as popular as the most popular choice?

   _____

3. Which flavor is the least popular?

   _____

4. Which flavor is the second most popular? _____

5. What is the mean, or average number, of votes? _____

1. Which school had the most volunteers in December? _____

   What was the total number of volunteers at that school for December? _____

2. How many more volunteers helped out from Mason than Garrett during the month of January? _____

3. Which school had the most volunteers in October? _____

4. Which month had the least total number of volunteers? _____

Line graphs and circle graphs
Unit 7

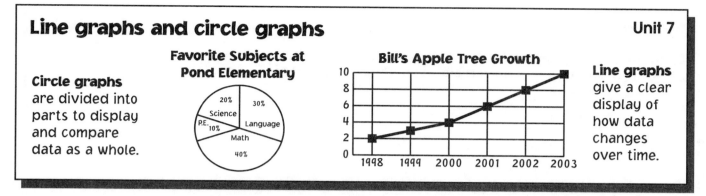

Circle graphs are divided into parts to display and compare data as a whole.

Favorite Subjects at Pond Elementary

20% Science
30% Language
P.E. 10%
Math
40%

Bill's Apple Tree Growth

Line graphs give a clear display of how data changes over time.

Use the graphs to answer each question.

Favorite Flower Colors

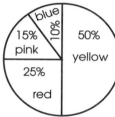

blue 10%
15% pink
50% yellow
25% red

1. Which color is the most popular? _____

2. Which color is the least popular? _____

3. Which color is half as popular as the most popular color? _____

4. Which two colors when combined equal the amount of popularity of the color red? _____

5. How much less popular is the color blue than the color yellow? _____

6. How much more popular is the color red than the color pink? _____

7. What percent of the circle graph do the four colors make? _____

8. What percent of the circle graph does not show the votes for the color blue? _____

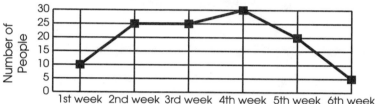

Singing Club Attendance

1. Which week had the highest attendance? _____

2. Between which two weeks was the greatest drop in attendance? _____

3. Between which two weeks was the greatest rise in attendance? _____

4. What was the total attendance for all six weeks? _____

5. Which week had the lowest attendance? _____

6. Which week did attendance begin to decline? _____

7. Between which two weeks did attendance stay the same? _____

8. What was the attendance for the first week? _____

9. What was the difference in attendance from week one to week two? _____

10. What was the difference in attendance from week one to week six? _____

11. What was the difference in attendance for the week with the most attendees and the week with the fewest attendees? _____

Probability

Probability is the likelihood that something will happen. You can show the probability that something will happen as a fraction.

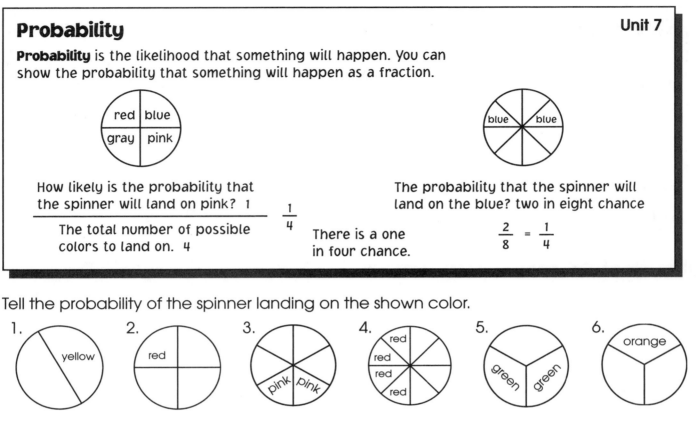

How likely is the probability that the spinner will land on pink? 1

The total number of possible colors to land on. 4

$\frac{1}{4}$

There is a one in four chance.

The probability that the spinner will land on the blue? two in eight chance

$\frac{2}{8} = \frac{1}{4}$

Tell the probability of the spinner landing on the shown color.

1. yellow

2. red

3. pink pink

4. red red red red

5. green green

6. orange

_____   _____   _____   _____   _____   _____

Tell the probability that Samuel's name will be chosen out of the bag.

7.   8.   9.   10.   11.

_____   _____   _____   _____   _____

Tell which color balloon is more likely to be chosen if the chooser is blindfolded when picking a balloon. Also, tell the probability of choosing that color balloon.

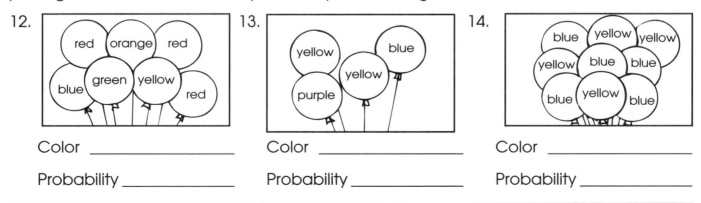

12. red orange red green yellow blue red

Color _____

Probability _____

13. yellow blue yellow purple

Color _____

Probability _____

14. blue yellow yellow yellow blue blue blue yellow blue

Color _____

Probability _____

Name

Read the question. Use an extra piece of paper
to write problems down and solve them.
Fill in the circle beside the best answer.

☐ Example:
   Add.

   14 min   51 s
   + 12 min   11 s

Ⓐ 26 min 2 s
Ⓑ 27 min 2 s
Ⓒ 28 min 2 s
Ⓓ NG

Take time to
review your
answers.

Answer: B because you regroup 60 seconds as 1 minute.

Now try these. You have 20 minutes. Continue until you see ⬡STOP⬡ .

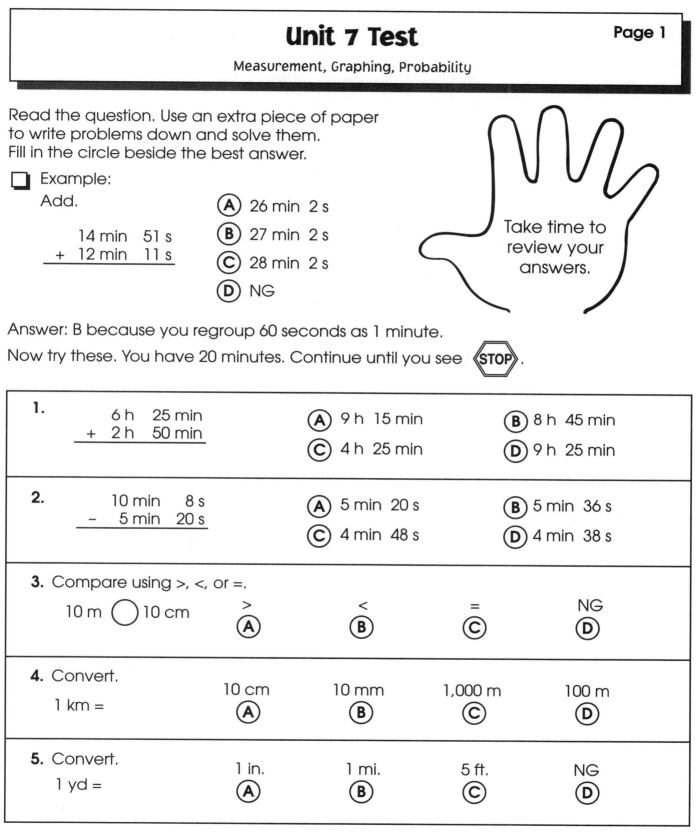

1.
     6 h   25 min
   + 2 h   50 min

Ⓐ 9 h 15 min   Ⓑ 8 h 45 min
Ⓒ 4 h 25 min   Ⓓ 9 h 25 min

2.
     10 min   8 s
   − 5 min   20 s

Ⓐ 5 min 20 s   Ⓑ 5 min 36 s
Ⓒ 4 min 48 s   Ⓓ 4 min 38 s

3. Compare using >, <, or =.

   10 m ◯ 10 cm

   >   <   =   NG
   Ⓐ   Ⓑ   Ⓒ   Ⓓ

4. Convert.

   1 km =

   10 cm   10 mm   1,000 m   100 m
   Ⓐ   Ⓑ   Ⓒ   Ⓓ

5. Convert.

   1 yd =

   1 in.   1 mi.   5 ft.   NG
   Ⓐ   Ⓑ   Ⓒ   Ⓓ

GO ON ▷

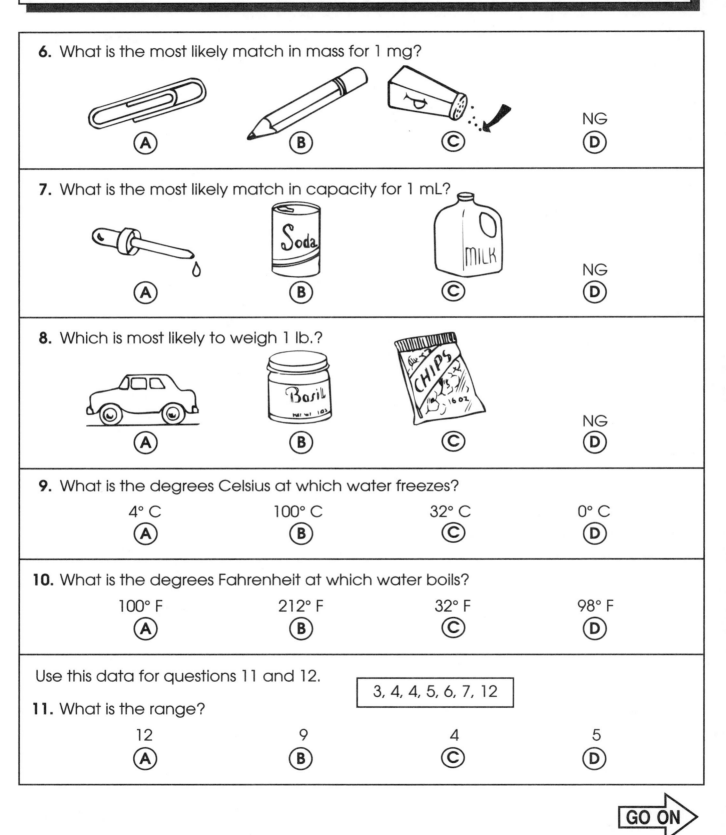

6. What is the most likely match in mass for 1 mg?

A   B   C   NG
                                 D

7. What is the most likely match in capacity for 1 mL?

A   B   C   NG
                                 D

8. Which is most likely to weigh 1 lb.?

A   B   C   NG
                                 D

9. What is the degrees Celsius at which water freezes?

4° C   100° C   32° C   0° C
A   B   C   D

10. What is the degrees Fahrenheit at which water boils?

100° F   212° F   32° F   98° F
A   B   C   D

Use this data for questions 11 and 12.

11. What is the range?

| 3, 4, 4, 5, 6, 7, 12 |

12   9   4   5
A   B   C   D

GO ON

Name _____

12. What is the median?

(A) 5   (B) 4   (C) 7   (D) 12

13. What is the mean? 1, 1, 2, 2, 2, 2, 3, 3

(A) 4   (B) 2   (C) 8   (D) 3

14. What mean equals 3?

(A) 6, 3, 1   (B) 5, 5, 5   (C) 4, 4, 1   (D) 2, 3, 9

Flowers Sold

Daisies	❀ ❀ ❀ ✿
Sunflowers	❀ ✿
Tulips	❀ ❀ ✿
Daffodils	❀ ❀

❀ = 10 flowers
✿ = 5 flowers

15. Which type of flower had a quantity of 25 flowers sold?

(A) daffodils   (B) tulips
(C) daisies   (D) sunflowers

16. Which day did Davey sell the most tacos?

(A) Monday   (B) Wednesday
(C) Thursday   (D) NG

Food Sold at Davey's Mexican Food Stand

enchiladas
tacos

Watermelon Choices

25% red seeded
70%
yellow seeded 5%
red seedless

17. Which type of watermelon is most popular?

(A) red seeded   (B) yellow seeded
(C) red seedless   (D) NG

GO ON

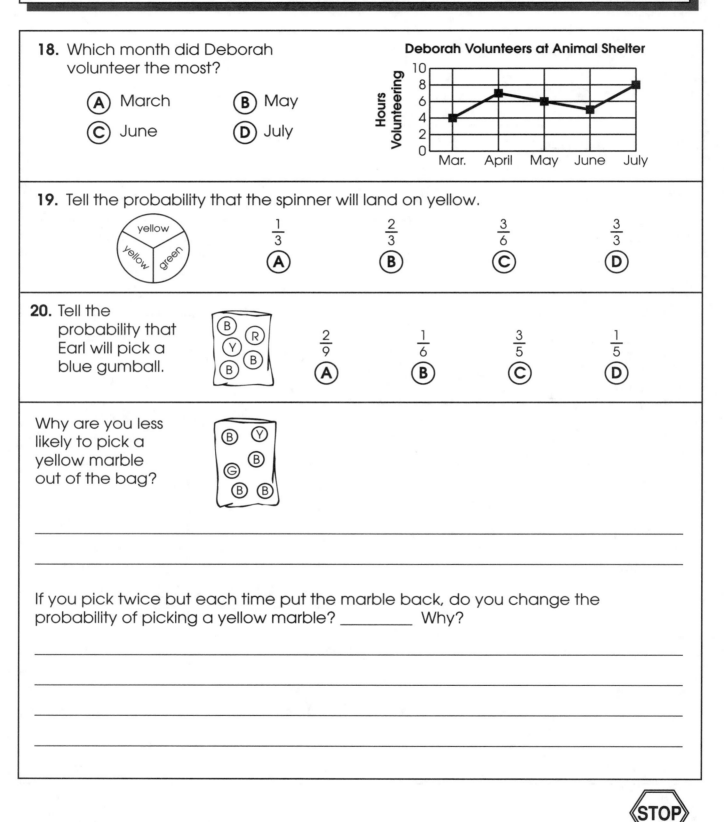

18. Which month did Deborah volunteer the most?

(A) March (B) May

(C) June (D) July

Deborah Volunteers at Animal Shelter

19. Tell the probability that the spinner will land on yellow.

$\frac{1}{3}$ (A) $\frac{2}{3}$ (B) $\frac{3}{6}$ (C) $\frac{3}{3}$ (D)

20. Tell the probability that Earl will pick a blue gumball.

$\frac{2}{9}$ (A) $\frac{1}{6}$ (B) $\frac{3}{5}$ (C) $\frac{1}{5}$ (D)

Why are you less likely to pick a yellow marble out of the bag?

_____

_____

If you pick twice but each time put the marble back, do you change the probability of picking a yellow marble? _____ Why?

_____

_____

_____

_____

STOP

104

Choosing the operation
Unit 8

When choosing the operation to apply to your problem, look for key words that can help you. Here are some examples to help develop a strategy to solve each problem.

Addition: What is the total, how many are there in all, or altogether? Example: Eva has $^1/_2$ of the pictures and David has $^1/_3$. What fraction of the pictures do they have altogether?

Subtraction: How many are remaining, what is the difference, how many are left? Example: His temperature was 100.6° F at 10:00 a.m. At 11:00 a.m. it dropped down to 98.6° F. What was the difference in his temperature when it dropped?

Multiplication: Look for the need to find the total for multiple groups. 3 x 6 really means, "the total for three groups of six." Example: There are 6 students in each science group. If there are 8 groups, what will be the total number of students involved in today's experiment?

Division: Look for the total given, and the need to find the amount in each group. Example: If 40 people come to the party, and we put 8 in each group, how many groups will there be?

Choose the operations. Then solve the problems.

1. Andy wants to invite 8 people from school to his party, 5 friends that he plays tennis with, and 19 friends that he knows through scouts. What is the total number of invitations that he needs to send out?

   Operation: _____   Answer: _____

2. A total of 80 students signed up for chorus. They were put into 4 equal groups to practice different parts. How many singers were in each group?

   Operation: _____   Answer: _____

3. Two-thirds of the students love to have pets in the classroom. One-eighth want to have more science experiments instead. How many more students want to have pets more than science experiments?

   Operation: _____   Answer: _____

4. Three different teachers want to take the field trip to the science museum. The cost is $324.12 for each class. What will be the total cost for all three groups to go?

   Operation: _____   Answer: _____

5. One-eighth of the students in Mr. Smile's class own rabbits. One-half own dogs. What fraction of the class own either rabbits or dogs?

   Operation: _____   Answer: _____

6. There are 4 schools in our town. Each school gets to have 800 free apples from the farm nearby. How many apples will be donated in all?

   Operation: _____   Answer: _____

Using a tree diagram

Unit 8

Sam and Steve love the sandwich shop near their house. They are trying to make up their minds between turkey and chicken sandwiches. The shop also gives a choice of having the sandwich made with whole wheat bread, a bagel, or a croissant. On top of that, it can be served hot or cold! Sam and Steve have a lot of choices to make. How many choices do they really have?

By setting up a **tree diagram**, you can easily find out.

Here's the choices they have altogether: 2 for the type of meat, 3 for the type of bread, and 2 for hot or cold. That is a total of 12 choices in all.

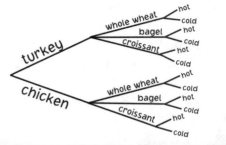

Draw tree diagrams to help you solve the following problems.

1. Gwen is so popular! She has three friends that have called today that want to get together. Heather wants to go ice skating or miniature golfing, Cheryl wants to go horseback riding or swimming, and Katelyn wants Gwen to come over and play with her new puppy or sing songs together. How many choices does Gwen have in all today?

2. Eric needs to buy a new bike helmet. He has two choices. There is the sleek new streamline look, or the regular basic helmet that most people have. Both helmets come in purple or blue. They also come in small, medium, and large sizes. How many choices does Eric have in making this decision?

3. Eva wants a new cat to play with after school. Her mom says that she can have the choice between either a Siamese or Persian breed. Also, she gets to decide between either a male or female. Lastly, she can have the option of getting a baby kitten, or an adult cat. How many choices does Eva have as she contemplates about her new cat?

4. Earl wants new paintbrushes for art class. At the store he sees that there are stiff bristles or soft. Also, there are extra long brushes or short. Lastly, there are wide, medium, and narrow brushes. How many choices does Earl have as he buys new brushes?

5. Uncle Jim and Aunt Joan want to come visit. They can come in either June or July. They have to decide if they want to fly or drive. Also, they have to make a decision if they want to stay in a hotel or at their nephew's house. How many decisions do Uncle Jim and Aunt Joan have altogether?

Name

Discovering patterns   Unit 8

By making a chart you can predict the results of a pattern.

Example: When Jose places 2 ice cubes in his glass, the temperature drops 4 degrees.
When he places 3 ice cubes in his glass, the temperature drops 6 degrees. As he
places 4 ice cubes in his glass, it drops 8 degrees. We can safely use a chart to
predict how many degrees it will drop when we place 12 ice cubes in his glass.

number of ice cubes	2	3	4	5	6	7	8	9	10	11	12
Drop in temperature	-4°	-6°	-8°	-10°	-12°	-14°	-16°	-18°	-20°	-22°	-24°

If the pattern continues, there will be a drop of 24 degrees!

Complete the charts to help you predict the outcomes of the following problems.

1. When Alexa sends one card in her envelope, it requires $.45 for postage. When she
    sends 2 cards in the mail, it requires $.90 for postage. If she sends 10 cards in the
    mail, how much will be required for postage? Complete the chart.

Number of Cards	1	2	3	4	5	6	7	8	9	10
Cost in Postage	$ .45	$ .90								

2. When first graders in our school have a pizza party, they eat an average of 1.2 slices
    each. Second graders eat an average of 1.5 slices each.
    Third graders eat an average of 1.8 slices each. If this pattern
    continues, what will be the average for fourth, fifth, and sixth
    grades? Complete the chart.

Grade Level	1st	2nd	3rd	4th	5th	6th
Average Slices Eaten	1.2	1.5	1.8			

3. It takes emergency vehicles 1.1 minutes travel time to
    arrive at a location that is 1 mile from the station. It
    takes an average of 2.2 minutes travel time to arrive at
    a location that is 2 miles from the station. If the
    emergency vehicle had to travel 10 miles, how many
    minutes would it take to get there? Complete the chart.

Distance in Miles	1	2	3	4	5	6	7	8	9	10
Travel Time in Minutes	1.1	2.2								

Using a table

Tables are helpful in organizing information.

Flour Needed for Monica's Famous Baked Dishes	
Baked chicken and vegetables	2 ½ c
Baked zucchini sticks with onions	1 ¾ c
Baked sausage and pepper	3 ⅛ c
Chicken stew and dumplings	2 ¼ c
Turkey pot pie	4 ⅛ c
Wheat germ blueberry muffins	2 ⁶⁄₈ c

Use the table to answer the questions.

1. How much more flour is needed to make turkey pot pie than baked zucchini sticks with onions? _____ c

2. How much flour is needed altogether to make baked sausage and pepper and baked chicken and vegetables? _____ c

3. Which takes more cups of flour to bake, turkey pot pie or wheat germ blueberry muffins? _____

4. How much less flour is needed to create chicken stew and dumplings than baked sausage and pepper? _____ c

5. How much total flour will be needed to create baked sausage and pepper, turkey pot pie, and wheat germ blueberry muffins? _____ c

6. How much more flour is needed to create turkey pot pie than baked chicken and vegetables? _____ c

7. Which will take more flour to create, turkey pot pie or baked chicken and vegetables combined with baked zucchini sticks with onions? _____
   _____

Multi-step problems   Unit 8

Figure the solution for multi-step problems one step at a time!

Example: The Wong Family is moving to Florida from California. They drive 400 miles on Monday, 500 miles on Tuesday, 450 miles on Wednesday, and 475 miles on Thursday. Did they travel a longer distance on Monday and Tuesday, or on Wednesday and Thursday?

Step one: Add the miles traveled on Monday and Tuesday. 400 m + 500 m = 900 m

Step two: Add the miles traveled on Wednesday and Thursday. 450 m + 475 m = 925 m

Step three: Compare the two sum totals. 900 m < 925 m

Use two or more steps to solve each problem.

1. Miriam painted 2 paintings each day for 5 days. Her father told her that he would pay her $2.00 for each painting. How much money did Miriam's father give her for painting those 5 days? _____ If she had painted an extra day, how much more would she have earned? _____

2. Manuel loves to sing in the choir. He never misses a rehearsal! Chung is always there, too. She loves to sing just as much as Manuel. They rehearse for 45 minutes each day on Monday, Tuesday, and Thursday. How many hours and minutes is that per week that they rehearse? _____

3. David's puppy gained 2 oz. in weight the first week at his house. The second week he gained 3 oz. The third week he gained an additional 4 oz. Which weeks did he gain more, the first and second combined, or the second and third combined?

_____

4. Ariol buys a hamburger and shake 3 times a week. The total he spends for the week is $7.35. How much does he spend each day? _____ How much would it cost to only buy hamburger and shakes 2 times a week? _____

5. One-third of the fifth graders like to play tether ball at recess. One-fourth of the sixth graders like to play. What fraction of the fifth and sixth graders like to play tether ball at recess? _____ What fraction of the fifth and sixth graders do not like to play tether ball at recess? _____

6. It takes 5 oz. of food each day to feed the rabbit in Mrs. Wolff's 5th grade class. It only takes 3.47 oz. each day to feed the hamsters. How many more ounces does it take per week to feed the rabbit than the hamsters?

_____

Too much information   Unit 8

1. Figure out which information is necessary to solve the problem.
2. Determine the operation.
3. Write a number sentence.
4. Solve.

Example: Benjamin pointed his telescope at a 130° and found Jupiter right away! Samuel pointed his telescope at 170° and located Saturn. Simon found Mars at 40°. How many more degrees towards the horizon did Samuel point his telescope than Benjamin?

1. Needed information: the angles of Benjamin and Samuel's telescopes
2. Operation: subtraction
3. Number sentence: 170 − 130 = 40
4. Answer: 40°

Solve.

1. The volume of Tammy's diorama was 500 in.³. The volume of Leandra's was 600 in.³. Shayla's diorama was actually 1,200 in.³, which is more than both of the others' combined. How much greater in volume was Leandra's diorama than Tammy's?

2. 18 people bought lemonade at Mark's lemonade stand on Saturday. The following Saturday Mark sold lemonade to 15 people. The Saturday after that Mark sold lemonade to 18 people. That was a total of almost 5 gallons of lemonade! What was the average number of people that bought lemonade each Saturday?

3. Marlene collected 4 ⅓ lb. of shells at the beach on Wednesday. Heather collected 3 ⅖ lb. Gusta collected 5 ²⁄₄ lb. of shells, but later gave them to her friend Sidel. What was the total pounds of shells that Marlene and Heather collected on Wednesday?

4. Levell and Cariton are the best of buddies! They love to run. They both ran 4.56 miles together on Monday after school. On Tuesday they ran 6 miles together! On Wednesday they ran 3.78 miles together, but decided not to run at all on Thursday or Friday. How many more miles did they run on Tuesday than Monday?

5. Max loves to build model airplanes. His sister Lilly does, too! Max spent 4.2 hours this week working on his latest model. Lilly spent 3.9 hours doing the same. They both also spent a total of 5 hours practicing piano. What is the total number of hours they spent building their models?

6. Roger has collected 32.5 oz. of salt by letting ocean water evaporate in a large tub that he owns. That is 5 times more than his friend Jim has collected. Tom has collected 3 times more than Roger. How much salt has Tom collected by evaporating ocean water?

Name

Using a picture

Unit 8

Sometimes a picture helps you solve problems. Remember that the shortest distance between two points is a straight path.

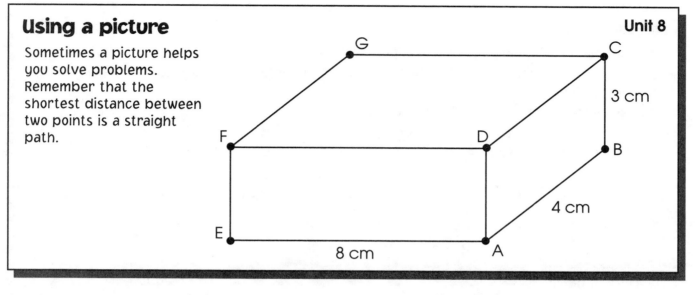

Answer the following questions using the rectangular prism above.

1. What is the shortest distance from point A to point F? Start at point A and travel to point _____, and go directly to point F. Distance: _____cm

2. If you are at point D, what is the shortest route to point B? Start at point D, travel to point _____, and go directly to point B. Distance: _____cm

3. What is the distance from point E to point B by way of point F, G, and C? Distance: _____cm

4. What is the distance from point B to point F by way of point A and E? _____cm

5. Circle the shorter route from point A to point B.
   A. By way of points E, F, G, and C. Distance: _____cm
   B. By way of points D and C. Distance: _____cm

6. Circle the shorter route from point E to point B?
   A. By way of points F, G, and C. Distance: _____cm
   B. By way of point A. Distance: _____ cm

7. What is the shortest route from point A to point C? Start at point A, go to point _____, and directly to point C. Distance: _____cm

8. What is a long route from point A to point B? You can only go through a point and path once. Start at point A, go to point _____, then to point _____, then to point _____, and then to point _____ and directly to point B. Hint: there are many answers that are correct for this question! Distance: _____ cm

Name

Equal ratios

When you want to increase something in an equal ratio, simply use the following formula.

Sarah needs 3 eggs for her egg sandwiches to feed 4 people. How many eggs does she need to feed 8 people?

Let's set up this formula to find the value of n:

$$\frac{3 \text{ eggs}}{4 \text{ people}} = \frac{n}{8 \text{ people}}$$

$$4 \times \boxed{} = 8$$

What do we multiply by 4 to equal 8?

$$4 \times 2 = 8$$

We multiply by 2.

$$\frac{3 \times 2}{4 \times 2} = \frac{n}{8}$$

Since we are creating an equal ratio, we multiply both numerator and denominator by 2.

$$\frac{3 \times 2}{4 \times 2} = \frac{6}{8}$$

$$n = 6 \text{ eggs}$$

Use the formula for equal ratios to find the value of n.

1. Emily has 3 pints of bubble soap for the 6 friends that she has invited to her party. Now she wants to invite 6 more friends. How many pints of bubble soap does she need?

2. Mr. Heigel will use 5 cups of corn starch for every 10 students to make his really fun oogle schnoogle mixture. If there are 30 students in his class, how many cups of cornstarch will he need?

3. It is pretzel day in Mrs. Ploeger's class today! Kimberly was told to place 2 pinches of salt for every 3 cups of flour that they mix together. If they use 12 cups of flour, how many pinches of salt will she need?

4. For every cup of water, Allison needs 4 drops of green food coloring for the math experiment they are going to do. How many drops will they need if they use 5 cups of water?

Name

Read the question. Use an extra piece of paper to write problems down and solve them. Fill in the circle beside the best answer.

☐ Example:

Choose the operation.

David has 14.5 lb. of bird seed to feed the birds outside. He is given another 30.2 lb. by his friends. How much bird seed does he have now?

(A) multiplication

(B) subtraction

(C) division

(D) NG

Note the time allotment. Pace yourself.

Answer: D because the operation is addition and it is not listed as a choice.

Now try these. You have 20 minutes. Continue until you see ⬡STOP⬡.

For problems 1 and 2, choose the operation.

1. Abby has a total of 40 apples from her tree to share. She wants to give each neighbor 5 apples. How many neighbors will she be able to be generous with her apples?

multiplication	subtraction	division	addition
(A)	(B)	(C)	(D)

2. Andy wants to share 25 pounds of food with the food bank near his house. He has already given them 40 pounds. How many pounds will he give them in all?

subtraction	division	addition	multiplication
(A)	(B)	(C)	(D)

GO ON ⟶

Use a tree diagram to solve problems 3–5.

3. Maria wants to buy a new dress. There are two different kinds that she can choose from, casual or fancy. Also, they each come in three different colors. On top of that, they come in cotton or polyester blend. How many choices does Maria have to think about?

12	10	16	7
Ⓐ	Ⓑ	Ⓒ	Ⓓ

4. Anthony wants to buy a lizard at the reptile shop. He has the choice between a chameleon or a gecko. Both come in baby and adult sizes. Lastly, each come in green or brown. How many choices does Anthony have to choose from in all?

6	12	8	10
Ⓐ	Ⓑ	Ⓒ	Ⓓ

5. Deborah's mom brought home some bagels for her family. There were four different types: whole wheat, cinnamon raisin, sesame seed, and cheddar cheese. Her mom said that she would serve them plain or toasted. Also, they could have them with or without cream cheese. How many actual choices does Deborah have as she gets ready to enjoy a bagel?

10	7	4	NG
Ⓐ	Ⓑ	Ⓒ	Ⓓ

Use the chart to answer questions 6–8.

Erica wants to have a lot of friends over for her slumber party. Her parents told her that she has to do 2 chores around the house for each friend that she invites. Use the chart to find out how many chores she will have to do for all the friends that she wants to have over.

Number of friends invited	1	2	3	4	5	6	7
Number of chores to do	2	4	6	8	10	12	14

GO ON ⟩

Unit 8 Test

6. If she has 3 friends over, how many chores will she have to do around the house?

    4 (A)   6 (B)   8 (C)   NG (D)

7. If Erica does 8 chores, how many friends will she be allowed to have over?

    2 (A)   4 (B)   6 (C)   16 (D)

8. If Erica decides to invite 7 friends, how many chores will she be doing?

    10 (A)   18 (B)   12 (C)   14 (D)

Refer to the table to answer questions 9–12.

Weekly Food Consumption for Each of Bill's Dog Friends	
Andy's dog	3 ¼ lb.
Monica's dog	2 ⅛ lb.
Chelsea's dog	4 ½ lb.
Roberta's dog	5 ¹⁄₁₆ lb.
Eldridge's dog	3 ⅞ lb.

9. How many pounds per week do Andy and Monica's dogs eat altogether?

    $5\frac{3}{8}$ (A) $6\frac{2}{4}$ (B) $5\frac{1}{4}$ (C) $7\frac{3}{4}$ (D)

10. Whose dog eats the most food in a week according to this chart?

    Eldridge's dog (A)   Andy's dog (B)   Chelsea's dog (C)   Roberta's dog (D)

GO ON

Unit 8 Test

11. How many more pounds per week does Roberta's dog eat than Eldridge's?

$8\frac{8}{16}$ $2\frac{6}{8}$ $1\frac{3}{16}$ $8\frac{15}{16}$

(A)   (B)   (C)   (D)

12. How many pounds per week do Roberta and Chelsea's dogs eat altogether?

$1\frac{1}{2}$ $9\frac{9}{16}$ $9\frac{2}{16}$ NG

(A)   (B)   (C)   (D)

13. Sela collected 7.5 oz. of hailstones during the storm on Monday. Tuesday she collected 6.3 oz. of hailstones. On Wednesday, there was an incredible downpour, and she collected 3 times as much as she had collected on Monday and Tuesday combined. How many ounces of hailstones did Sela collect on Wednesday?

41.4 oz.   25.6 oz.   13.8 oz.   16.8 oz.

(A)   (B)   (C)   (D)

14. Aaron drew 20 drawings this month. Last month he drew 30. He gave an equal amount of drawings to each of 5 brothers. How many drawings did each of his brothers get?

20   30   10   4

(A)   (B)   (C)   (D)

15. Samantha's room is 12 ft. long and 10 ft. wide. She has two doors to her room. How many square feet does her room contain?

22 ft.^{2} 120 ft.^{2} 24 ft.^{2} 100 ft.^{2}

(A)   (B)   (C)   (D)

16. Mary's aquarium is 4 ft. long, 1 ft. wide, and 2 ft. high. It is on a table that is 3 feet off the ground. What is the volume of the aquarium in cubic feet?

8 ft.^{3} 12 ft.^{3} 6 ft.^{3} NG

(A)   (B)   (C)   (D)

GO ON

Unit 8 Test

Use the picture to answer questions 17 and 18.

17. What is the distance from point E to point D by way of points A and B?

(A) 8 cm   (B) 12.6 cm

(C) 10.3 cm   (D) 13.5 cm

18. What is the distance from point F to point C by way of points E and A?

(A) 10.6 cm   (B) 11.5 cm

(C) 8 cm   (D) 9.1 cm

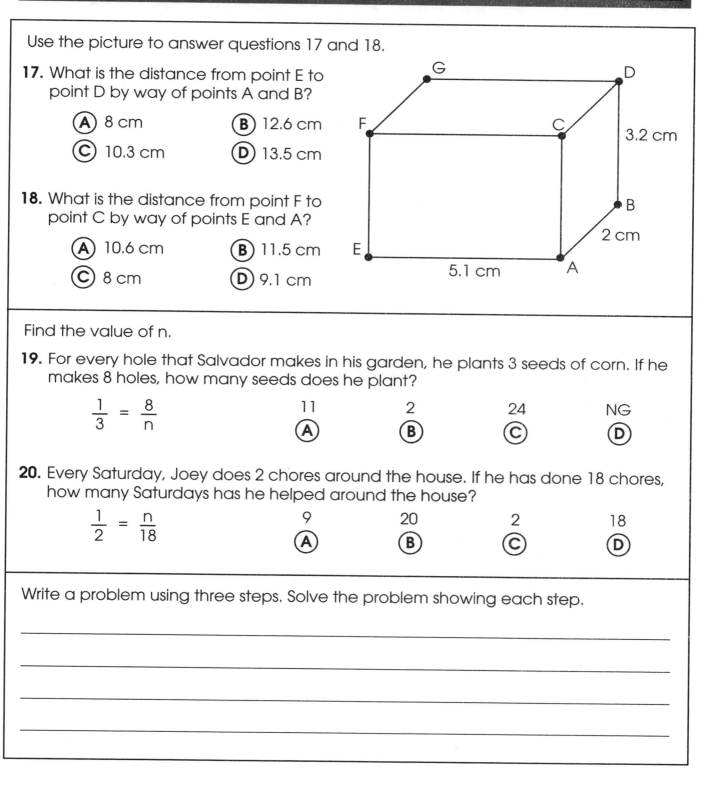

Find the value of n.

19. For every hole that Salvador makes in his garden, he plants 3 seeds of corn. If he makes 8 holes, how many seeds does he plant?

$$\frac{1}{3} = \frac{8}{n}$$

11 (A)   2 (B)   24 (C)   NG (D)

20. Every Saturday, Joey does 2 chores around the house. If he has done 18 chores, how many Saturdays has he helped around the house?

$$\frac{1}{2} = \frac{n}{18}$$

9 (A)   20 (B)   2 (C)   18 (D)

Write a problem using three steps. Solve the problem showing each step.

_____

_____

_____

_____

Final Review Test Name Grid

Write your name in pencil in the boxes along the top. Begin with your last name. Fill in as many letters as will fit. Then follow the columns straight down and bubble in the letters that correspond with the letters in your name. Complete the rest of the information the same way. You may use a piece of scrap paper to help you keep your place.

STUDENT'S NAME		SCHOOL
LAST / FIRST / MI		TEACHER

FEMALE ○   MALE ○

DATE OF BIRTH

MONTH	DAY	YEAR
JAN ○	⓪ ⓪	⓪ ⓪
FEB ○	① ①	① ①
MAR ○	② ②	② ②
APR ○	③ ③	③ ③
MAY ○	④	④ ④
JUN ○	⑤	⑤ ⑤
JUL ○	⑥	⑥ ⑥
AUG ○	⑦	⑦ ⑦
SEP ○	⑧	⑧ ⑧
OCT ○	⑨	⑨ ⑨
NOV ○		
DEC ○		

GRADE ③ ④ ⑤

(Name grid bubbles A–Z for each letter column)

Final Review Test Answer Sheet

Pay close attention when transferring your answers. Fill in the bubbles neatly and completely. You may use a piece of scrap paper to help you keep your place.

SAMPLES
A Ⓐ Ⓑ ● Ⓓ
B Ⓕ ● Ⓗ Ⓙ

1 Ⓐ Ⓑ Ⓒ Ⓓ	7 Ⓐ Ⓑ Ⓒ Ⓓ	13 Ⓐ Ⓑ Ⓒ Ⓓ	19 Ⓐ Ⓑ Ⓒ Ⓓ	25 Ⓐ Ⓑ Ⓒ Ⓓ
2 Ⓕ Ⓖ Ⓗ Ⓙ	8 Ⓕ Ⓖ Ⓗ Ⓙ	14 Ⓕ Ⓖ Ⓗ Ⓙ	20 Ⓕ Ⓖ Ⓗ Ⓙ	26 Ⓕ Ⓖ Ⓗ Ⓙ
3 Ⓐ Ⓑ Ⓒ Ⓓ	9 Ⓐ Ⓑ Ⓒ Ⓓ	15 Ⓐ Ⓑ Ⓒ Ⓓ	21 Ⓐ Ⓑ Ⓒ Ⓓ	27 Ⓐ Ⓑ Ⓒ Ⓓ
4 Ⓕ Ⓖ Ⓗ Ⓙ	10 Ⓕ Ⓖ Ⓗ Ⓙ	16 Ⓕ Ⓖ Ⓗ Ⓙ	22 Ⓕ Ⓖ Ⓗ Ⓙ	28 Ⓕ Ⓖ Ⓗ Ⓙ
5 Ⓐ Ⓑ Ⓒ Ⓓ	11 Ⓐ Ⓑ Ⓒ Ⓓ	17 Ⓐ Ⓑ Ⓒ Ⓓ	23 Ⓐ Ⓑ Ⓒ Ⓓ	29 Ⓐ Ⓑ Ⓒ Ⓓ
6 Ⓕ Ⓖ Ⓗ Ⓙ	12 Ⓕ Ⓖ Ⓗ Ⓙ	18 Ⓕ Ⓖ Ⓗ Ⓙ	24 Ⓕ Ⓖ Ⓗ Ⓙ	30 Ⓕ Ⓖ Ⓗ Ⓙ

Read the question. Use an extra piece of paper to write problems down and solve them. Fill in the circle beside the best answer.

Remember your Helping Hand Strategies:

Example:

Round $367.45 to the nearest hundred dollars.

(A) $300.00
(B) $370.00
(C) $400.00
(D) NG

Answer: C

Now try these. You have 30 minutes.

Continue until you see ⬡STOP .

1. Cross out answers you know are wrong.

2. Always read the question twice. Does your answer make sense?

3. Take time to review your answers.

4. Fill in the answer circle completely and neatly.

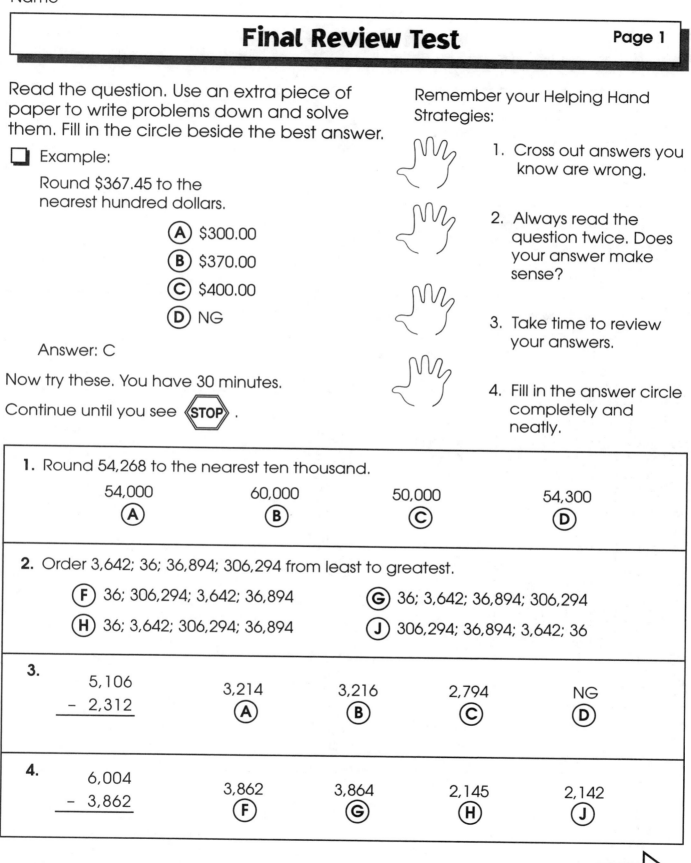

1. Round 54,268 to the nearest ten thousand.

| 54,000 | 60,000 | 50,000 | 54,300 |
| (A) | (B) | (C) | (D) |

2. Order 3,642; 36; 36,894; 306,294 from least to greatest.

(F) 36; 306,294; 3,642; 36,894   (G) 36; 3,642; 36,894; 306,294

(H) 36; 3,642; 306,294; 36,894   (J) 306,294; 36,894; 3,642; 36

3.

5,106
− 2,312

| 3,214 | 3,216 | 2,794 | NG |
| (A) | (B) | (C) | (D) |

4.

6,004
− 3,862

| 3,862 | 3,864 | 2,145 | 2,142 |
| (F) | (G) | (H) | (J) |

GO ON ➡

Name

Final Review Test

5.

3,168
x   5

15,168 Ⓐ   15,840 Ⓑ   15,488 Ⓒ   15,500 Ⓓ

6.

$24.59
x   8

$150.59 Ⓕ $180.59 Ⓖ $196.72 Ⓗ $162.02 Ⓙ

7. What is the value of n? 6 x n = 8 x 6

8 Ⓐ   6 Ⓑ   48 Ⓒ   NG Ⓓ

8.

3,000
x   30

3,00030 Ⓕ   90,000 Ⓖ   9,000 Ⓗ   30,000 Ⓙ

9.

5) 727

129 R6 Ⓐ   140 R7 Ⓑ   145 R2 Ⓒ   154 R4 Ⓓ

10.

6) $16.68

$2.78 Ⓕ $5.68 Ⓖ $4.25 Ⓗ   NG Ⓙ

11.

34) 272

7 Ⓐ   9 Ⓑ   6 Ⓒ   8 Ⓓ

GO ON

Final Review Test

12. What is incorrect in this division problem?

```
       22 R10
   8 ) 186
     - 16
       26
     - 16
       10
```

(F) There is a mistake in subtracting.

(G) The difference of "10" is greater than the divisor—needs a larger digit in the quotient.

(H) The remainder is in the wrong spot.

(J) NG

13. Convert $4\frac{62}{100}$ to a decimal.

462.00   (A)   46.2   (B)   4.62   (C)   0.462   (D)

14. Add. $6.4 + 31.2 + 0.521$

38.121   (F)   37.521   (G)   31.62   (H)   8.97   (J)

15.
```
     8
 - 2.314
```
6.314   (A)   6.796   (B)   5.686   (C)   10.314   (D)

16.
```
   132.5
 x   0.8
```
180.40   (F)   832.40   (G)   105.84   (H)   NG   (J)

17. A flat surface that extends out unending in all directions is a:

line   (A)   ray   (B)   plane   (C)   point   (D)

Final Review Test

18. Identify.

rhombus
(F)

hexagon
(G)

pentagon
(H)

octagon
(J)

19. Using the formula $A = (b \times h) \div 2$, find the area.

4 mm

8 mm

16 mm^2
(A)

32 mm^2
(B)

4 mm^2
(C)

12 mm^2
(D)

20. Identify.

2 cm

radius
(F)

diameter
(G)

chord
(H)

NG
(J)

21. Reduce $\frac{18}{24}$ to lowest terms.

$\frac{9}{12}$
(A)

$\frac{6}{8}$
(B)

$\frac{3}{4}$
(C)

$\frac{1}{2}$
(D)

22.

$\frac{3}{10}$
$+ \frac{5}{20}$

$\frac{8}{20}$
(F)

$\frac{11}{20}$
(G)

$\frac{8}{10}$
(H)

NG
(J)

23.

$8\frac{1}{3}$
$- 5\frac{5}{6}$

$2\frac{1}{2}$
(A)

$3\frac{5}{6}$
(B)

$3\frac{4}{6}$
(C)

$13\frac{1}{6}$
(D)

24. Tell the probability of the spinner landing on 8.

$\frac{2}{6}$
(F)

$\frac{4}{8}$
(G)

$\frac{5}{6}$
(H)

$\frac{4}{6}$
(J)

GO ON

25.

$$\begin{array}{ll} 10 \text{ min} & 38 \text{ s} \\ + \ 15 \text{ min} & 41 \text{ s} \end{array}$$

(A) 25 min 70 s

(B) 26 min 19 s

(C) 24 min 79 s

(D) 25 min 19 s

26. Find the range for this set of data: 3, 4, 8, 12, 18, 23

26 (F)   25 (G)   20 (H)   12 (J)

27. Find the mean for this set of data: 2, 6, 8, 12, 12

8 (A)   12 (B)   2 (C)   6 (D)

28. Divide. Use the diagram. $5 \div \frac{1}{3} =$ _____

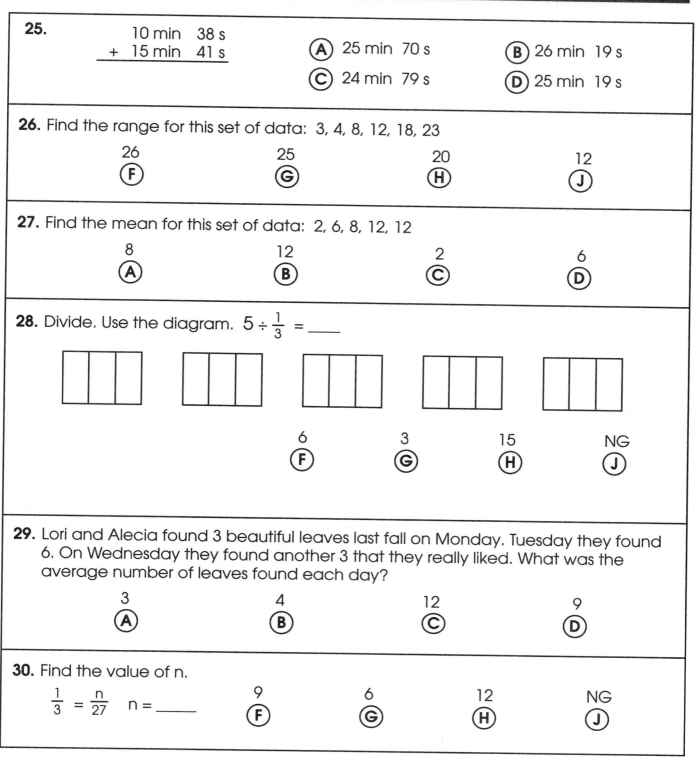

6 (F)   3 (G)   15 (H)   NG (J)

29. Lori and Alecia found 3 beautiful leaves last fall on Monday. Tuesday they found 6. On Wednesday they found another 3 that they really liked. What was the average number of leaves found each day?

3 (A)   4 (B)   12 (C)   9 (D)

30. Find the value of n.

$\frac{1}{3} = \frac{n}{27}$ n = _____

9 (F)   6 (G)   12 (H)   NG (J)

GO ON

Final Review Test

Tell three things that you learned from this book that you never knew before.

1. _____

2. _____

3. _____

Give an example in your own words how you have used math learned from this book in your everyday life.

_____

_____

_____

_____

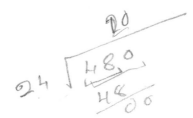

Teach & Test Math: Grade 5